In: Criminal Justice, Law Enforcement and Corrections

Mass Incarceration and Offender Reentry in the United States

CRIMINAL JUSTICE, LAW ENFORCEMENT AND CORRECTIONS

Homicide Investigations
Allan B. Smythe
2009 ISBN 978-1-60692-258-3

Mass Incarceration and Offender Reentry in the United States
Russell D. Javitze
2009 ISBN 978-1-60692-657-4

In: Criminal Justice, Law Enforcement and Corrections

MASS INCARCERATION AND OFFENDER REENTRY IN THE UNITED STATES

RUSSELL D. JAVITZE
EDITOR

Nova Science Publishers, Inc.
New York

For permission to use material from this book please contact us:
Telephone 631-231-7269; Fax 631-231-8175
Web Site: http://www.novapublishers.com

LIBRARY OF CONGRESS CATALOGING-IN-PUBLICATION DATA
Available upon Request
ISBN: 978-1-60692-657-4

Published by Nova Science Publishers, Inc. ✢ New York

CONTENTS

Preface		**vii**
Chapter 1	Offender Reentry: Correctional Statistics, Reintegrationinto the Community, and Recidivism *Blas Nuñez-Neto*	**1**
Chapter 2	Mass Incarceration in the United States: At What Cost? *U.S. Government Printing Office*	**55**
Index		**153**

PREFACE

America's incarceration rate raises several serious questions. These include: The correlation between mass imprisonment and crime rates; the impact of incarceration on minority communities and women; the economic costs of the prison system; criminal justice policy; and transitioning ex-offenders back into their communities and into productive employment. Equally important, the prison system today calls into question the effects on our society at a broad level. The combined expenditures of local, State, and Federal governments for law enforcement and corrections personnel now total over $200 billion. Prison construction and operations has become a sought after, if uncertain, tool of economic growth for rural communities. Are there ways to spend less money, enhance public safety, and make a fairer prison system? Having such a large prison population also has significant employment and productivity implications. The economic output of prisoners is mostly lost to society while they are in prison. These negative productivity effects continue in many cases after release.

Chapter 1 - The prison population in the United States has been growing steadily for more over 30 years. The Bureau of Justice Statistics reports that each year more than 65 0,000 offenders are released into the community and almost 5 million ex-offenders are under some form of community-based supervision. Offender reentry can include all the activities and programming conducted to prepare ex-convicts to return safely to the community and to live as law-abiding citizens. Some ex-offenders, however, eventually end up back in prison. The most recent national-level recidivism study is 10 years old; this study showed that two-thirds of ex-offenders released in 1994 came back into contact with the criminal justice system within three years of their release. Compared with the average American, ex-offenders are less educated, less likely to be gainfully employed, and more likely to have a history of mental illness or substance abuse — all of which have been shown to be risk factors.

Three phases are associated with offender reentry programs: programs that take place during incarceration, which aim to prepare offenders for their eventual release; programs that take place during offenders' release period, which seek to connect ex- offenders with the various services they may require; and long-term programs that take place as ex-offenders permanently reintegrate into their communities, which attempt to provide offenders with support and supervision. There is a wide array of offender reentry program designs, and these programs can differ significantly in range, scope, and methodology. Researchers in the offender reentry field have suggested that the best programs begin during incarceration and extend throughout the release and reintegration process. Despite the relative lack of research in the field of offender reentry, an emerging "what works" literature has shown that programs focusing on work training and placement, drug and mental health treatment, and housing assistance have proven to be effective.

The federal government's involvement in offender reentry programs typically occurs through grant funding, which is available through a wide array of federal programs at the Departments of Justice, Labor, Education, and Health and Human Services. However, only a handful of grant programs in the federal government are designed explicitly for offender reentry purposes.

The 110th Congress is considering a number of bills that include some form of offender reentry program within their purview. The Second Chance Act (P.L. 110-199) was enacted on April 9, 2008. The Act expands the current offender reentry grant program at the Department of Justice and creates a wide array of targeted grant- funded pilot programs. Bills pertaining to offender reentry include S. 1060, S. 2237, S. 456, S. 1907, H.R. 623, H.R. 3187, H.R. 3547, H.R. 3467, and H.R. 3409. Potential issues facing Congress include the adequacy of the federal government's existing grant programs, the lack of current national-level statistics on recidivism, whether other outcome measures should be considered, whether more funding should be allocated toward program evaluations, and whether enough coordination is taking place among the various federal agencies that manage programs used to fund offender reentry. This report will be updated as circumstances dictate.

Chapter 2 – Hearing before the Joint Economic Committee, Congress of the United States. One Hundred Tenth Congress First Session October 4, 2007.

The Committee met at 10:04 a.m. in room 216 of the Hart Senate Office Building, the Honorable Jim Webb and Vice Chair Carolyn B. Maloney, presiding.

Senators present: Webb, Casey, and Brownback. Representatives present: Maloney, English, Scott, and Hin-chey.

Staff present: Christina Baumgardner, Stephanie Dreyer, Chris Frenze, Nan Gibson, Gretta Goodwin, Rachel Greszler, Colleen Healy, Aaron Kabaker, Israel Klein, Michael Laskawy, Zachary Luck, Robert O'Quinn, Jeff Schlagenhauf, and Robert Weingart.

In: Mass Incarceration and Offender Reentry in U.S. ISBN 978-1-60692-657-4
Editor: Russell D. Javitze, pp. 1-53

Chapter 1

OFFENDER REENTRY: CORRECTIONAL STATISTICS, REINTEGRATION INTO THE COMMUNITY, AND RECIDIVISM*

Blas Nuñez-Neto

ABSTRACT

The prison population in the United States has been growing steadily for more over 30 years. The Bureau of Justice Statistics reports that each year more than 65 0,000 offenders are released into the community and almost 5 million ex-offenders are under some form of community-based supervision. Offender reentry can include all the activities and programming conducted to prepare ex-convicts to return safely to the community and to live as law-abiding citizens. Some ex-offenders, however, eventually end up back in prison. The most recent national-level recidivism study is 10 years old; this study showed that two-thirds of ex-offenders released in 1994 came back into contact with the criminal justice system within three years of their release. Compared with the average American, ex-offenders are less educated, less likely to be gainfully employed, and more likely to have a history of mental illness or substance abuse — all of which have been shown to be risk factors.

Three phases are associated with offender reentry programs: programs that take place during incarceration, which aim to prepare offenders for their eventual release; programs that take place during offenders' release period,

* Excerpted from CRS RL34287, dated July 11, 2008.

which seek to connect ex- offenders with the various services they may require; and long-term programs that take place as ex-offenders permanently reintegrate into their communities, which attempt to provide offenders with support and supervision. There is a wide array of offender reentry program designs, and these programs can differ significantly in range, scope, and methodology. Researchers in the offender reentry field have suggested that the best programs begin during incarceration and extend throughout the release and reintegration process. Despite the relative lack of research in the field of offender reentry, an emerging "what works" literature has shown that programs focusing on work training and placement, drug and mental health treatment, and housing assistance have proven to be effective.

The federal government's involvement in offender reentry programs typically occurs through grant funding, which is available through a wide array of federal programs at the Departments of Justice, Labor, Education, and Health and Human Services. However, only a handful of grant programs in the federal government are designed explicitly for offender reentry purposes.

The 110th Congress is considering a number of bills that include some form of offender reentry program within their purview. The Second Chance Act (P.L. 110- 199) was enacted on April 9, 2008. The Act expands the current offender reentry grant program at the Department of Justice and creates a wide array of targeted grant- funded pilot programs. Bills pertaining to offender reentry include S. 1060, S. 2237, S. 456, S. 1907, H.R. 623, H.R. 3187, H.R. 3547, H.R. 3467, and H.R. 3409. Potential issues facing Congress include the adequacy of the federal government's existing grant programs, the lack of current national-level statistics on recidivism, whether other outcome measures should be considered, whether more funding should be allocated toward program evaluations, and whether enough coordination is taking place among the various federal agencies that manage programs used to fund offender reentry. This report will be updated as circumstances dictate.

BACKGROUND

Over 95% of the prison population today will be released at some point in the future, and each year in the United States almost 650,000 offenders are released from prison [1]. The Department of Justice's (DOJ) Bureau of Justice Statistics (BJS) has estimated that two-thirds of all released prisoners will commit new offenses (recidivate) within three years of their release [2]. Many studies have indicated that reentry initiatives that combine work training and placement with counseling and housing assistance can reduce recidivism rates [3]. According to the BJS, the average per prisoner cost of incarceration in state prison in 2001 was $62 per day, or $22,650 per year; costs for those incarcerated in federal prison was similar. Overall, the states spent $38 billion on their correctional systems in 2001, the most recent year for which data are available [4].

Offender reentry includes all the activities and programming conducted to prepare ex-convicts to return safely to the community and to live as law-abiding citizens. Reentry programs are typically divided into three phases: programs that prepare offenders to reenter society while they are in prison, programs that connect ex-offenders with services immediately after they are released from prison, and programs that provide long-term support and supervision for ex-offenders as they settle into communities permanently. Offender reentry programs vary widely in range, scope, and methodology. The best-designed programs, according to the research in the field, are those that span all three phases [5].

A Government Accountability Office (GAO) report also suggests that post-release planning should begin as early as possible, ideally as soon as an inmate is admitted into prison or even immediately after sentencing. Such planning could include helping the offender to develop the skills and knowledge base necessary to find a well-paying job and have access to education, such as General Equivalency Degree classes for those who have not completed high school, and either vocational training or college classes for those that have completed high school but have not settled on a career [6].

As offenders approach their release date, the research suggests that reentry planning focus on connecting offenders with the community and workplace resources they will need to get established. Again, employment and access to education has been cited by many studies as two of the most important aspects contributing to the successful reintegration of ex-offenders into society [7]. Lastly, it is important for the reentry process to extend deep into the offenders' reintegration into society. Indeed, for many offenders, the first few weeks of adjustment after release are actually less difficult than the longer period of community reintegration [8]. In many cases, this period of time can span the entire three to five years that offenders are sometimes supervised in the community [9].

CORRECTIONAL SYSTEM STATISTICS

To understand the issue of offender reentry, one must first understand the ways in which ex-offenders are released into the community. It is also worthwhile to analyze the population of individuals serving sentences in correctional facilities, because the number of offenders re-entering the community is necessarily related to the number of offenders serving prison sentences. This section analyzes national data on the nation's correctional system.

Population in Correctional Facilities

The correctional system includes two main forms of detention: jails and prisons. Jails, also known as local lockups, are facilities generally used to temporarily detain individuals who have been arrested or charged with a crime but not usually convicted [10]. The jail population is thus extremely fluid, with individuals usually staying for a matter of weeks, and includes individuals who may never be convicted of a crime. Prisons, on the other hand, typically house individuals who have been convicted of a crime and sentenced to a term of one year or longer. For this reason, the prison population is less fluid than the jail population [11].

Over 95% of offenders currently serving prison sentences will return to the community at some point [12]. The population serving time in correctional facilities has been steadily increasing for decades, reaching a peak of almost 2.2 million in 2005. Of the 2.2 million prison population, 93% were between the ages of 20 and 54 [13]. From 1995 to 2005, the population of prisoners aged 20 to 54 increased by 35% — or three and a half times the average growth in the general population aged 20-54 during this period of 10% [14]. From 1995 to 2005, the number of people imprisoned in the United States increased by roughly 3% each year, compared with the overall population growth of roughly 1% each year. According to the United Kingdom's Home Office, it appears that the United States incarcerates more of its citizens than any other nation in the world, at 701 per 100,000 of its population in 2002. More than 60% of countries in the British survey, including most European countries, imprisoned less than 150 per 100,000 [15]. Figure 1 shows the annual population in state and federal correctional facilities in 1995 and 2000-2005.

Given the fact that 95% of all inmates will eventually return to the community, the prison population has a direct impact on offender reentry. As the prison population grows, increasing numbers of ex-offenders are being released from correctional facilities. Most of these ex-offenders are required to undergo some form of community supervision as part of their release. The following section explores the mechanisms and statistics surrounding the release of prisoners into the community.

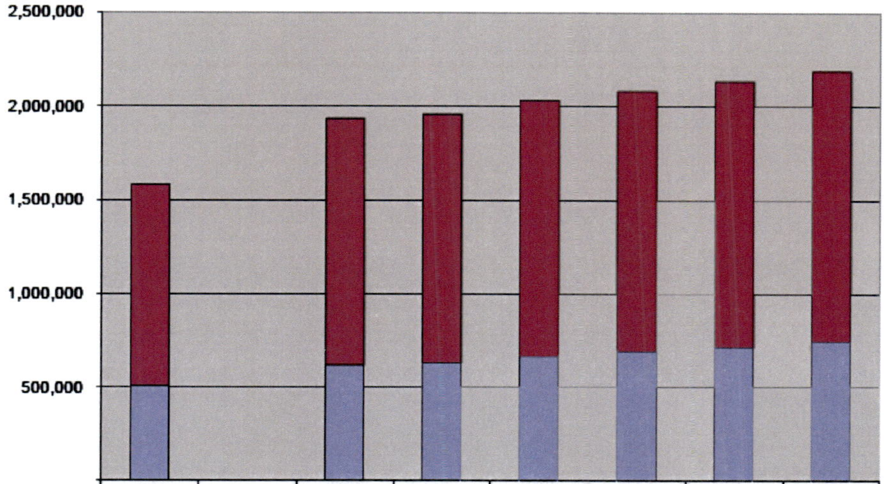

	1995		2000	2001	2002	2003	2004	2005
Prison	1,078,542		1,316,333	1,330,007	1,367,547	1,390,279	1,421,911	1,446,269
Jail	507,044		621,149	631,240	665,475	691,301	713,990	747,529

Source: CRS analysis of Bureau of Justice Statistics data.

Figure 1. Annual Population in Federal and State Correctional Facilities.

EX-OFFENDERS UNDER COMMUNITY SUPERVISION

Ex-offenders can be released into the community through a variety of different mechanisms. Some offenders never serve prison sentences and instead serve their sentence on probation in their communities under supervision. Others serve most of their sentences in correctional facilities but are then released on parole to finish their sentences in their communities under supervision. Lastly, some offenders serve out their entire sentences in correctional facilities and are released unconditionally into the community.

Probation. Individuals who are found guilty of committing a crime that is deemed not serious enough for imprisonment can be sentenced to serve their sentences under community supervision (probation). Offenders on probation typically must adhere to certain conditions and check in regularly with their probation officers. Violation of these conditions or failure to appear before their probation officers can lead to further criminal sanctions, including incarceration. In some instances, offenders can be sentenced to a mixed term of prison and probation.

Parole [16]. Individuals who have served most of their sentences in a correctional facility are sometimes eligible to complete their sentences in the community under conditional supervision. The conditions associated with parole can vary from case to case, but typically include drug testing and regular contact with a parole officer. Violations of these conditions can result in the parolee returning to prison to serve out the remaining portion of his or her sentence. There are two different kinds of parole: discretionary and mandatory.

Ex-offenders can be released into the community through a variety of different mechanisms. Some offenders never serve prison sentences and instead serve their sentence on probation in their communities under supervision. Others serve most of their sentences in correctional facilities but are then released on parole to finish their sentences in their communities under supervision. Lastly, some offenders serve out their entire sentences in correctional facilities and are released unconditionally into the community.

Discretionary Parole. States that use parole boards to determine whether a prisoner should be released into the community have discretionary parole. The parole boards have the authority to conditionally release a prisoner into the community based on a statutory or an administrative determination that the prisoner is eligible.

Mandatory Parole. States that have statutory language determining when offenders should be released into the community have mandatory parole. Jurisdictions that use determinate sentencing [17] often include provisions specifying when inmates should be conditionally released from prison after serving a specified portion of their original sentences.

Figure 2 shows the number offenders being supervised in the community, either through probation or through parole. It is important to note that parolees account for, on average, 16% of the overall population under community supervision. The growing state prison population has resulted in a concomitant growth in the overall population of offenders under community supervision. Interestingly, however, the growth rate of individuals under community supervision has been lagging behind the growth rate of individuals in correctional facilities. This is likely due to the fact that a growing number of offenders are being released directly into the community without any form of supervision. Figure 2 shows that the average population of individuals under community supervision has increased by 32% from 1995 to 2005; this contrasts with the overall prison population, shown in Figure 1, which grew by 38% during this period. From 2000 to 2003, the overall population under supervision increased at a relatively steady rate of 2.5% per year, which corresponded with the annual growth in prison population over the same three-year period.

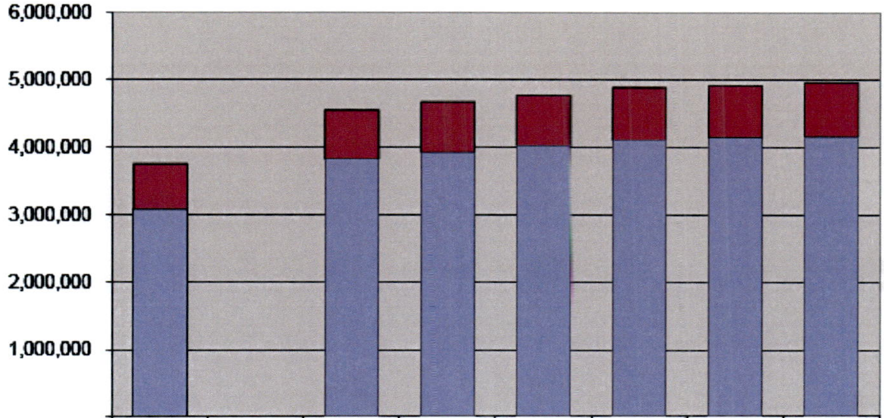

	1995		2000	2001	2002	2003	2004	2005
Parole	679,421		723,898	732,333	750,934	769,925	771,852	784,408
Probation	3,077,861		3,826,209	3,931,731	4,024,067	4,120,012	4,143,466	4,162,536

Source: CRS analysis of Bureau of Justice Statistics data.

Figure 2. Population Under Federal andState Community Supervision.

However, for reasons that are not altogether clear, in 2004 and 2005, the growth in the population under community supervision slowed to 0.6% a year; this contrasts with the 3% average growth in the prison population over this period (see Figure 1). This recent disparity in the annual growth rate of the parole and prison populations suggests that the disconnect between the growth in the overall prison population and the growth in the overall population under community supervision may continue to widen in the short term.

Figure 3 breaks out the annual state parole entries and the year-end [18] state parole population each year from 1980 through 2005 [19]. The data show that the growth rate in the states' parole populations has declined over the last 14 years for which data are available. From 1980 through 1992, the year-end parole population more than tripled to 618,689. From 1992 through 2005, however, the population of ex-offenders on parole has increased by only 12% to 693,197 — an average increase of about 0.9% each year. In addition, from 2000 to 2005, the number of entries into the parole population has slightly exceeded the number of exits from parole each year, although both entries and exits to parole have been increasing by about 1.7% annually. This could suggest that offenders are remaining on parole for longer periods of time, or that the parole population is growing relative to the number of people being released from prison.

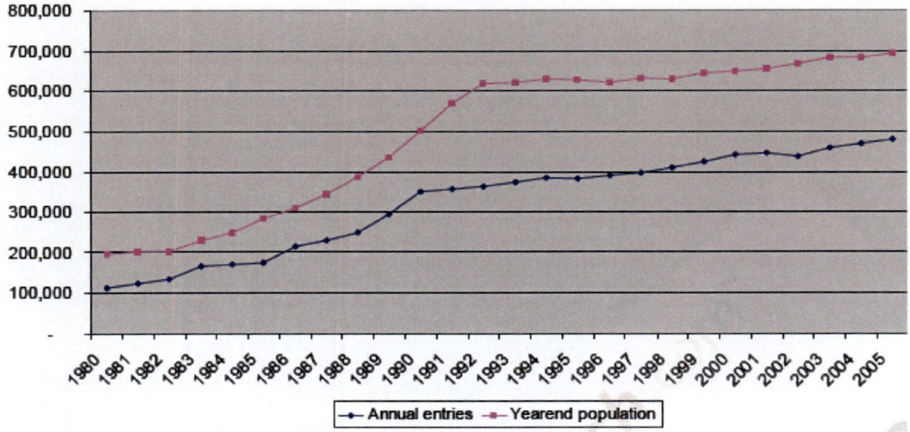

Source: CRS analysis of Bureau of Justice Statistics data.

Figure 3. Annual State Parole Entries and Year-End Population.

The relationship between the prison and parole populations is an important one for a number of reasons. Offenders serving their sentences in prison have committed more serious crimes than offenders who serve their sentences in jail or on probation; as previously noted, the prison population typically includes individuals sentenced to more than a year of time. Parolees, meanwhile, often return to the community after a prolonged period of incarceration and usually face a period of adjustment.

Figure 4 shows the relationship between annual changes in the state prison population and the parole population. Figure 4 shows a differentiation between the period from 1981 to 1992, when the annual increase in the state parole population generally outstripped the annual increase in the prison population, and the period from 1993 to 2005, when the obverse has largely been true. This is interesting for a number of reasons. The population of offenders on parole is, by definition, a subset of the population of offenders in prison: to get parole, one has to pass through the prison system. The fact that the population in prison has been increasing at a faster rate than the population in parole over the past 13 years suggests that fewer prisoners are being released before the end of their sentences; this corresponds with the sentencing reform efforts implemented by many states in the 1980s and early 1990s and the growing use of truth-in-sentencing laws by states. Truth-in-sentencing laws require that offenders serve a substantial portion of their sentences (usually three quarters), thereby reducing discrepancies between the sentence imposed and the actual time served in prison [20].

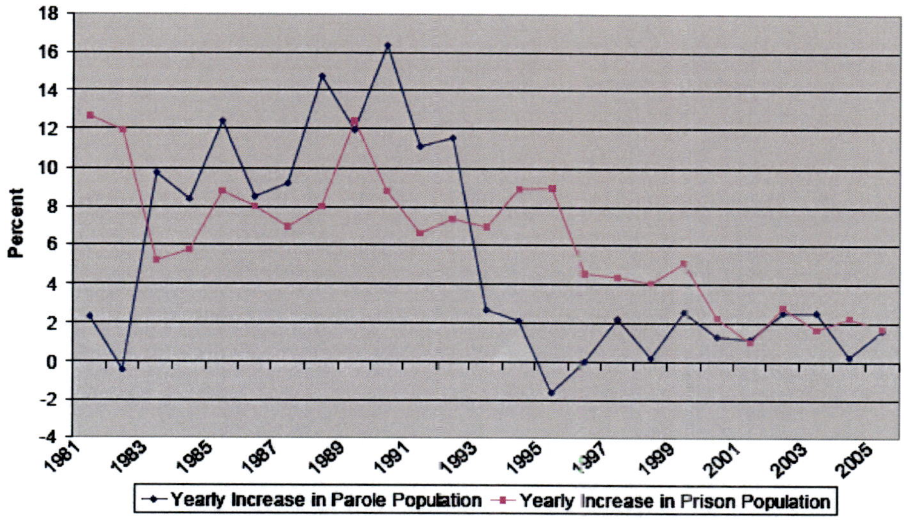

Source: CRS analysis of Bureau of Justice Statistics data.

Figure 4. Annual Increases in State Parole and Prison Populations.

The discrepancy between the annual growth of the parole and prison populations in the 1990s is also a result of the fact that prison sentences have been becoming longer, because of the enactment by most states of mandatory minimum sentencing laws. Taken together, these factors could suggest that the parole population may begin to grow faster than the prison population in coming years as the longer sentences that have been issued over the past two decades come closer to being completed.

The data analyzed thus far have examined the relationship between the prison population and the population under community supervision, revealing that the population of offenders under some form of community supervision accounts for roughly 70% of the overall population of offenders. Only 30% of offenders are in jail or prison, leaving about 5 million offenders annually in the community under probation or parole. As seen here, the number of offenders under community supervision has been increasing steadily for decades but has not grown quite as fast as the incarcerated population. Many of these individuals will end up recidivating and entering the penal system again, either during their periods of supervision or once their sentences have been completed.

Figure 5 below shows the types of releases from state prisons from 1980 to 2005. It shows the kinds of reentries that have been occurring historically and reveals that the vast majority of prisoners are released into some form of community supervision.

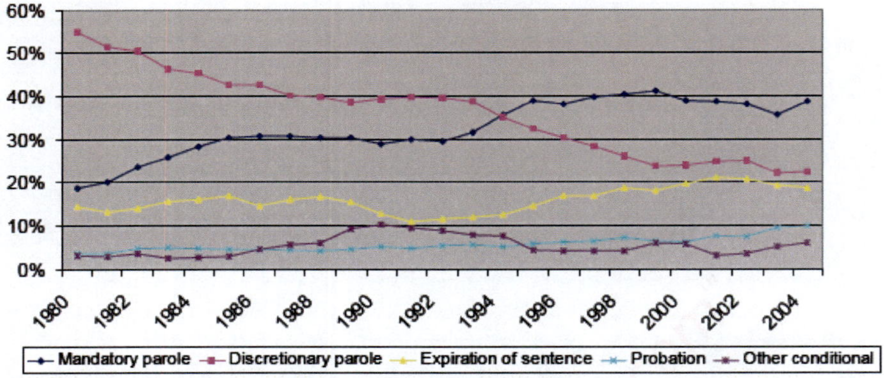

Source: CRS adaptation of Bureau of Justice Statistics figure.

Note: Other conditional releases include provisional releases, supervised work furloughs, releases to home arrest or boot camp programs, conditional pardons, conditional medical releases, or unspecified releases.

Figure 5. Types of Releases from State Prisons.

The figure also reflects the structural change in state systems from the use of discretionary parole (e.g., parole boards) toward mandatory parole (e.g., statutorily mandated parole) over the past 25 years. The number of individuals being released into probation has been increasing over the past 25 years, from about 4% in 1980 to 10% in 2005, but nevertheless remains relatively small. In addition, Figure 5 shows that the number of individuals being released directly into the community as their sentences expire has been increasing, from roughly 11% in 1991 to an average of 20% over the past five years. This means that roughly 20% of all offenders are being released into the community without any form of supervision or structured reentry and could account for the lower growth rate in the population of ex-offenders being supervised in the community compared with the growth rate of the prison population.

The figures presented above paint a picture of a correctional system that has been expanding in terms of population for over two decades. In turn, the number of individuals being released from prison into the community has been expanding as well. Figure 5 demonstrates some of the structural changes that have occurred in the reentry process over the past two and a half decades, namely the increasing use of mandatory parole and the decreasing use of discretionary parole as a result of the sentencing reforms that have occurred at the state level. Figure 5 also shows that the percentage of prisoners being released into the community with no form of direct supervision has been increasing until recently, averaging 20% of all releases over the past five years. Despite a slight downturn over the past three years, this trend has clear implications for offender reentry, given that ex-offenders released without any form of supervision may have difficulty connecting to the services and programs that exist in their communities and may be more prone to recidivating.

Recidivism

Recidivism is often defined as the rearrest, reconviction, or reincarceration of an ex-offender within a given time frame. As a result of this broad definition of recidivism, most studies include technical violations of an offender's parole or probation (such as failing a drug test or not showing up for a meeting, for example) within their general recidivism statistics. Rearrest statistics also include individuals who are found innocent of the charges. For these reasons, some studies have focused on reincarceration with a new prison sentence as a more accurate recidivism statistic, arguing that technical violations are really an extension of an offender's original prison term and not a newly committed crime. Essentially, there are two competing philosophies about what recidivism should mean [21]. On the one hand are those who argue that any new contact with the criminal justice system, no matter how minor, should be considered recidivism on the part of an ex-offender [22]. On the other hand are those who argue that recidivism should be more narrowly defined as the commission of a new crime, resulting in a new sentence, by an ex-offender [23]. What one includes in the definition of recidivism has a substantial impact on the rate of recidivism reported.

Regardless of what definition is used, recidivism is a difficult subject to study. Tracking recidivism involves following the cases of individuals for a number of years and relying on state or national level data sets that contain inherent inaccuracies. For example, if an offender is released in California but commits a new crime in Maine, the researchers must be able to match those two records together to make a definitive statement about recidivism. This match is typically done by consulting the FBI's master database of convictions; however, as we will see later, this database contains omissions that may affect the results of recidivism studies. A number of studies have been conducted on this issue, and most states have calculated their own recidivism rates. However, there is a dearth of current national-level statistics on recidivism by ex-offenders. The two main national level studies that have been conducted over the last 15 years are outlined below.

Bureau of Justice Statistics 1994 Recidivism Study. The most comprehensive national-level recidivism study to date was conducted by the Bureau of Justice Statistics (BJS) and dates back to 1994 [24]. The BJS study examined the rearrest, reconviction, and reincarceration of prisoners from 15 states three years after their release in 1 994 [25]. The study tracked 272,111 prisoners, or almost two-thirds of all the prisoners released from state prisons in 1994.

Figure 6 below summarizes the main findings of the BJS recidivism study. After three years, the study found that over two-thirds (67.5%) of the prisoners released had been rearrested for a new offense. Almost half (46.9%) of the prisoners had been reconvicted of a new crime. Just over half (51.8%) of the prisoners released were back in prison either because they had been resentenced to prison for a new crime they had committed (25.4%) or because they had violated some technical provision of their release (26.4%) [26].

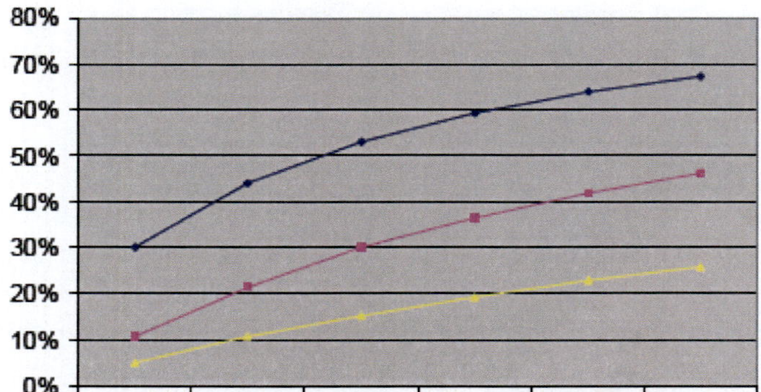

	6 months	12 months	18 months	24 months	30 months	36 months
Rearrested	30%	44%	53%	59%	64%	67%
Reconvicted	11%	22%	30%	36%	42%	46%
Returned to prison with a new prison sentence	5%	11%	15%	19%	23%	26%

Source: CRS analysis of Bureau of Justice Statistics data.

Notes: Because of missing data, prisoners released in Ohio were excluded from the calculation of "Percent reconvicted." The category "New prison sentence" includes sentences to state and federal penitentiaries but does not include sentences to local jails. Because of missing data, prisoners released in Ohio and Virginia were excluded from the calculation of "Percent returned to prison with a new prison sentence."

Figure 6. Bureau of Justice Statistics Recidivism Study.

The BJS study therefore showed that more than half of ex-offenders who return to prison do so because of technical violations of their parole or probation rather than the commission of a new crime. It is important to note that the BJS study did not include information on what percentage of ex- offenders were serving time in local jails; however, as previously noted, local jails feature a fluid population of inmates who usually reside there for a brief period of time and may not be convicted of the crime they are being held for.

United States Sentencing Commission Study. The United States Sentencing Commission (USSC) studied the recidivism rates of a random sample of 6,062 offenders who were sentenced under federal sentencing guidelines in FY1992. The recidivism information was derived from the "RAP" sheet criminal history repository maintained by the FBI's Criminal Justice Information Services Division, which has certain limitations (discussed below). The USSC study examined the relationship between the offenders' sentences and recidivism rates. The USSC developed the Criminal History Category (CHC) based on a review of prediction measures that were popularized in a National Academy of Sciences study in the 1980s [27]. Generally, an offender's prior criminal record will determine which CHC they are placed in. There are six CHC levels; an offender's placement within these levels is determined by a points system based on their prior contacts with the criminal justice system. Points are awarded for prior convictions, for violations of technical provisions of their judicial supervision (e.g., bail or parole), and for violent crimes. Juvenile and special court martial convictions are also counted. The higher the category, the more severe the offender's criminal history is [28].

Figure 7 summarizes the USSC's findings. Generally, the study showed that an offender's criminal history was strongly associated with the likelihood of the offender recidivating after being released. The more prior convictions or the more serious the nature of the offender's crimes, the more likely the offender was to recidivate. The study also showed that the definition of recidivism had a large impact on the resulting statistics. For example, for the most hardened ex-offenders, general recidivism, which includes any contact with the criminal justice system, was at 55% after two years. Over this same period, the re-conviction rate for the most hardened ex-offenders was only 15%. This discrepancy shows that the definition of recidivism is important; even for the most hardened ex-offenders, the reconviction rate was relatively low compared with the general recidivism.

National Recidivism Study Limitations. The rearrest, reconvition, and resentencing data used in both the USSC and the BJS study come from official records maintained by the states' and the Federal Bureau of Investigation's (FBI) official criminal history repositories.

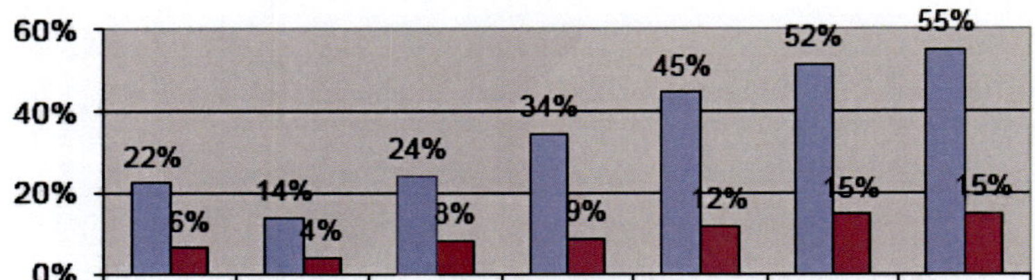

	Total	Category 1	Category 2	Category 3	Category 4	Category 5	Category 6
General Recidivism	22%	14%	24%	34%	45%	52%	55%
Re-Conviction	6%	4%	8%	9%	12%	15%	15%

General Recidivism Re-Conviction

Source: CRS presentation of United States Sentencing Commission data.

Figure 7. United States Sentencing Commission Recidivism Findings.

These repositories understate the actual recidivism levels to some unknown extent because they rely on local police agencies and courts to supply them with notifying documents. These documents are not always filed by local police departments or courts, however. In addition, if the offender provided a different name or a fraudulent identity document to police, and this misinformation was not discovered, they would likely not be captured by the data. Lastly, even if the criminal is correctly identified and the document is sent to the repository, the repository may not be able to match the person identified in the document with their records. This could occur, for example, if the document that has been submitted is filled out incorrectly or is illegible.

Moreover, as previously noted, there is some debate about what kind of outcome measure should be included when measuring recidivism. Should recidivism statistics include any contact with the criminal justice system by an ex-offender? Or should recidivism statistics be limited to the commission of crimes by ex-offenders that result in new convictions or new sentences? Both the BJS and the USSC studies showed wide differentials between general recidivism, which includes any contact with the criminal justice system, and re-conviction rates for new crimes. The length of the follow-up period will also play a role in the recidivism statistics that are generated. Because of the costs and difficulties associated with studying recidivism, most studies follow ex-offenders for two or three years. There is a dearth of information concerning what happens to ex-offenders beyond the three-year window that is typically studied.

For all of these reasons, caution should be taken when attempting to draw conclusions about the efficacy of policy measures based solely on recidivism statistics. When using recidivism statistics to evaluate a program, it is important to understand exactly what is included in the definition of recidivism. For example, consider the following hypothetical scenario: a program is evaluated and shows significant decreases in the number of ex-offenders that are convicted of new crimes and sentenced to new prison terms; however, the number of ex-offenders arrested for violating their parole actually increased. Was this program successful or not? Did it make society safer or not? This may well be an unlikely scenario, but it calls attention to the fact that recidivism may mean different things to different people. While recidivism statistics remain the best information available concerning whether ex-offenders come into contact with the criminal justice system after being released from prison and what the nature of that contact is, they are but one factor to be considered when evaluating the efficacy of a program, because of the concerns outlined above.

Importance of Considering Other Outcome Measures. While recidivism has traditionally been the most widely used metric used to determine the effectiveness of correctional and reentry programs, it is important to note here that other outcome measures can help determine whether an offender's reintegration into society is succeeding. Measures of attachment to social institutions, such as employment, involvement in community activities, church-going, and participation in support groups, can be important bellwethers of an offender's transition to the community [29]. For example, one study of drug court [30] participants showed that drug courts reduce drug use among their participants and that children born to drug court participants are less likely to be born addicted to drugs [31]. Given the high societal costs associated with substance-dependent infants, for that particular program, recidivism was arguably not the most important outcome measure that could have been considered. To give policy makers a better idea of what happens to ex- offenders, program evaluations are best focused on the entire universe of activities that ex-offenders engage in.

OFFENDER REENTRY: A BRIEF LITERATURE REVIEW

Virtually all prisoners currently being detained in secure facilities will, someday, be released into the community, and more offenders are transitioning into the community today than ever before. Offender reentry is a complex issue that touches on a wide range of social and governmental networks and programs. Offender reentry policies can vary significantly from state to state, and from community to community within particular states. The policies affecting prisoners and the kinds of programs available to them both in and out of prison depend on a variety of factors, including the availability of funding for social programs within states and communities and the number of private non-profit and religious organizations operating in a given community. The federal government plays a supporting role through the numerous grant funding opportunities (discussed below). Complicating factors affecting how offender reentry works in a given community can include

- the varying types of sentences handed down,
- the different kinds of release mechanisms available to judges,
- the types of programs provided in prisons by correctional systems,
- the intensity of supervision provided or required by the parole or releasing agency,
- the family and community support available to the offender,
- the kinds of social services available in the offender's community, and
- the status of the local economy and the offender's ability to obtain employment [32].

Offender Reentry Defined

Before we can discuss offender reentry programs, however, we must understand what constitutes offender reentry. Some observers note that offender reentry is the natural byproduct of incarceration, because all prisoners who are not sentenced to life in prison and who do not die in prison will reenter the community at some point. According to this school of thought, reentry is not a program or some kind of legal status but rather a process that almost all offenders will undergo [33]. A variant on this approach to reentry is the concept that offender reentry, "simply defined, includes all activities and programming conducted to prepare ex-convicts to return safely to the community and to live as law abiding citizens" [34]. The basic idea here is that every activity and process that a prisoner undergoes while in the judicial and correctional systems will have some nexus with their reentry into the community.

Although this broad definition of reentry certainly encompasses all the activities that may impinge on or affect a prisoner's reentry into society, it may be a cumbersome one for the purposes of crafting and evaluating government policies. For example, it is difficult, if not impossible, to measure the outcome of a reentry program if one includes in the definition of reentry every activity that a prisoner undergoes during his time in the criminal justice system. This has led many in the field to focus on a more narrow and thus more manageable definition of reentry. This more narrow definition is often stated in two parts: correctional programs that focus on the transition to the community (such as prerelease, work release, halfway houses, or other programs specifically aiming at reentry) and programs that have initiated some form of treatment (such as substance abuse, life skills, education, or mental health) in prison that is linked to community programs that will continue the treatment once the prisoner has been released [35]. Narrowing the definition of reentry thusly allows policy makers to focus on programs that expressly aim to manage the transition from detention to the community.

Program Effectiveness: The "What Works" Literature

Compared with other social science fields, there has been a relative lack of rigorously designed studies on the issue of offender reentry. Nevertheless, in recent years, there has been increasing attention on this issue and a number of new studies have been published. This has allowed academics to undertake some of the first broad meta-analyses [36] of offender reentry studies. Some of these studies have hewn closely to the "what works" paradigm created by University of Maryland researchers for a National Institute of Justice report to Congress [37]. This concept was adapted to the field of offender reentry in a 2003 St. Louis University Study [38]. The "what works" literature attempts to identify programs that are effective by creating a scoring system to evaluate studies based on whether they can be proven to have an impact. Inherent to this approach is the need to identify program evaluations that provide evidence concerning the effect the program had on certain outcome measures. The "what works" paradigm essentially focuses on whether studies have accomplished the following things:

- controlled for variables in their analysis that may have been the underlying cause of any observed connection between the program being studied and the outcome measures being analyzed;
- determined whether there are measurement errors resulting from problems with the study, including such things as participants being lost over time or low response rates to interview requests; and
- calculated the statistical power of the analysis to detect the program's effects on outcome measures. Included in this category are things such as sample size and the base rate of crime in the community [39].

The "what works" model uses these core criteria to place studies into five distinct categories, with category 5 being the most scientifically rigorous, and thus considered most effective, studies. The model then uses this criteria to identify programs that, based on the evidence considered, have been proven to work, programs that are promising, and programs that do not work.

Following is a brief discussion of the types of offender reentry programs that have been found to be effective in the "what works" literature, as well as in other studies. It is important to note here that, just because a program has been proven to work in one location, or for a certain population, does not necessarily mean that it can be just as effective in other locations or among other populations. A number of factors can impinge on a program's effectiveness in any given location. For example, while knowing that a program has worked in the past can provide a model or blueprint to guide policy practitioners in other locations, how a program is implemented is just as important to its ultimate success as the underlying model that it is based on. The most effective model program can be compromised if it is not implemented properly. In addition, geographic, demographic, and other differences between locations can affect whether a program that succeeded in one place succeeds in another. Nevertheless, knowing that a program has worked in the past is of use to policy makers as they consider where to allocate funding and other resources.

Employment. There are a number of studies that demonstrate that employment is a fundamental component of the reentry process, and that ex- offenders who are able to find stable employment are much more likely to succeed in their rehabilitation than those who cannot find work [40]. Several vocational and work programs were found to effectively reduce recidivism and improve the job-readiness of ex-offenders by the "what works" review [41].

Drug Treatment. Drug rehabilitation and treatment have also been found to be effective by a number of different studies, including the "what works" literature. These studies showed that, for recidivism and drug-use relapse, drug treatment can significantly improve outcome measures. In general, programs that provide intensive treatment in prison, combined and integrated with aftercare programs, have been shown to be effective in reducing recidivism and substance abuse among their participants — especially for offenders with serious crime and substance abuse histories [42].

Halfway House Programs. A number of programs that provide transitional housing for ex-offenders as they begin their transition into the community have been found to be effective. Offenders participating in halfway house programs were found to commit fewer and less severe offenses than those who did not participate. Participants also performed better on a range of other outcome measures, such as finding and holding a job, being self-supporting, and participating in self- improvement programs; however, these results were not statistically significant [43].

Other Kinds of Programs. The "what works" review concluded that other programs were either not effective or had not been studied enough for firm conclusions to be drawn. Education programs, for example, were found to raise educational achievement scores but not to reduce recidivism. Pre-release programs and programs focusing on violent offenders and sex offenders showed some evidence that they were effective in reducing recidivism, but few of these kinds of studies made it through the selection process. This precluded any firm conclusions from being drawn about these kinds of programs and pointed to the need for more evaluations [44].

Limitations with the "What Works" Literature. One of the main limitations associated with the "what works" literature is the dearth of studies that meet its rigorous requirements. For example, the offender reentry study cited above was only able to identify 32 studies that met their selection criteria. Only 19 of these program evaluations contained a comparison, or control, group, and of these, only two were randomized control trials [45]. This has led some to question whether the programs identified to work by this literature review are, in fact, effective [46]. Moreover, most of the studies identified by the "what works" literature evaluate program effectiveness based almost entirely on recidivism. As previously noted, some believe other outcome measures may be just as important in deciding whether a program has been effective in reintegrating ex-offenders into their communities. Lastly, evaluations that incorporate random assignment and provide statistically rigorous results are, by and large, expensive. This means that policy makers are often confronted with hard decisions concerning whether to fund additional services or evaluations of existing programs.

Conclusions. After reviewing the available literature, some patterns appear to emerge. Many of the programs that have been proven to be effective share some of the same attributes, regardless of whether they focus on vocational training, substance abuse prevention, mental health services, or alternative housing. The attributes shared by most of these programs include the following:

- they start during institutional placement, but take place mostly in the community;
- they are intensive in nature, lasting typically at least six months;
- they focus services on individuals determined to be at high-risk of recidivating through the use of risk-assessment classifications; and

- if they are treatment programs, they use cognitive-behavioral treatment techniques, matching particular therapists and programs to the specific learning characteristics of the offenders [47].

CURRENT LAW

The federal government's only grant program exclusively focused on offender reentry was authorized by the 21st Century Department of Justice Reauthorization Act of 2002 [48]. The act authorizes the Attorney General (AG) to make grants of up to $1 million to states, territories, and Indian tribes to fund adult and juvenile offender reentry demonstration projects. Funding can be used to provide the following services for adults:

- oversight and monitoring of offenders released into the community,
- substance abuse and mental health treatment and aftercare,
- vocational training and education,
- convening community and victim impact panels and educational classes,
- establishing and implementing graduated sanctions and incentives, and
- "other treatment to promote effective reintegration into the community."

Purpose areas eligible for funding for juvenile offender reentry are largely similar to those listed above, but also include providing offender reentry planning when the juvenile is initially incarcerated and coordinating the delivery of community-based services post-release.

To be eligible for funding, applicants to these demonstration grants must describe their long-term strategy, including how the jurisdiction will pay for the program once federal funding ends, and identify the governmental and community agencies that will be coordinated by the project. Applicants must also describe the methodology and outcome measures that will be used to evaluate the program. The federal share of any grant issued may not exceed 75% of the costs of the project; however, the AG is authorized to waive this requirement. This program was last authorized through FY2005; this means that it is currently unauthorized. However, this grant program has continued to receive funding.

In addition to the offender reentry demonstration grant program outlined above, purpose areas that can be used to fund offender reentry programs at the state and local level exist in a large number of federal grant programs. The following section provides an overview of the current programs that can include some funding for offender reentry purposes.

FEDERAL OFFENDER REENTRY PROGRAMS

A wide array of federal programs and grants can be used by states to support offender reentry. Many of these programs participated in the federal government-wide Serious and Violent Offender Reentry Initiative (SVORI), a four-year $300 million initiative that pooled the federal offender reentry resources of the Departments of Justice, Labor, Education, and Housing and Urban Development in order to reduce recidivism [49]. This program officially concluded in FY2005 and is currently being evaluated. More recently, the Office of Justice Programs (OJP) announced it had formed a partnership with the Department of Labor known as the Prisoner Reentry Initiative (PRI). The PRI program, like SVORI, is an interagency effort to coordinate the provision of federal funding for the reintegration of offenders into the community. While funding opportunities for offender reentry programs exist within the purpose areas of many broad grant programs, only one grant program is (PRI) specifically tailored for offender reentry within the federal government. Both the SVORI and the PRI utilized the authorization outlined above; however, as previously noted, the authorization expired in FY2005 but the program has continued to receive appropriations in FY2006 and FY2007. Following is a brief description of the main federal programs that have been used to help state and local entities to fund activities relating to the reintegration of ex-offenders into local communities. It is important to note that some of these programs may no longer be receiving funding; these programs are identified below. Other programs that are currently funded may not provide funding for offender reentry purposes every fiscal year. Nevertheless, these programs have been included to provide a comprehensive look at the universe of federal resources that could be used for offender reentry purposes.

Offender Reentry Programs at the Department of Justice (DOJ)

The Office of Justice Programs within DOJ oversees a wide array of grant programs that include support for offender reentry programs or activities among the purpose areas eligible for funding. Some of these programs may be more focused on offender reentry than others, but all of them can be used for offender reentry purposes.

Table 1. Direct Appropriations for DOJ Reentry Grant Programs

Fiscal Year	Appropriation	Public Law	Conference Report
FY2001	$30,000,000	P.L.106-553	H.Rept. 106-1005
FY2002	$14,934,000	P.L.107-77	H.Rept. 107-278
FY2003	$14,934,000	P.L.108-7	H.Rept. 108-10
FY2004	$5,000,000	P.L.108-199	H.Rept. 108-401
FY2005	$10,000,000	P.L. 108-447	H.Rept. 108-576
FY2006	$8,000,000b	P.L. 109-208	H.Rept. 109-272
FY2007	$7,897,600c	P.L. 110-5	N/A
FY2008	$11,750,000	P.L. 110-161	House Appropriations Committee Print
FY2009 (Request)	— [d]	N/A	N/A

Note: As previously noted, DOJ replaced the SVORI program with the PRI program in FY2006; however as both of these grant programs were implemented under the authority granted by the reentry program codified at 42 U.S.C. 3797w, they have been combined in this table. It is important to note as well that reentry funding has been appropriated in other federal agencies' budgets. a. Department of Justice, 2006 Congressional Authorization and Budget Submission, p. Office of Justice Programs 17. b. In FY2006, there was also $5 million appropriated for reentry grant programs under the Office of Justice Programs and $3 million appropriated for faith-based reentry programs under the Federal Prison Service. These totals have been combined in this table, but it should be noted that they are for different programs. c. The FY2007 appropriation is based on FY2006 enacted minus a 1.28% rescission, as per P.L. 110-5. d. The FY2009 President's request for the Prisoner Reentry Initiative would eliminate the program, consolidating its funding and purpose areas into a large discretionary grant program known as the Byrne Public Safety and Protection Program.

The Serious and Violent Offender Reentry Initiative. The Office of Justice Programs (OJP) coordinated a federal offender reentry pilot program for adult offenders, the Serious and Violent Offender Reentry Initiative (SVORI). This program focused on coordinating the way federal agencies distribute existing offender reentry funding. The main federal agencies involved were the Departments of Justice, Labor, Education, and Housing and Urban Development. As part of SVORI, their objective was to help state and local agencies navigate the wide array of existing state formula and block grants and to assist the states and communities to leverage those resources to create comprehensive offender reentry programs. The program distributed $110 million to 69 grantees and concluded in FY2005; it is currently being evaluated [50].

The Prisoner Reentry Initiative. The Prisoner Reentry Initiative (PRI) appears to have been instituted as a replacement for the SVORI program. According to OJP, the PRI provides funding for model offender reentry programs that focus on providing services and assistance during the three phases of offender reentry: at detention facilities, just prior to and after the offender's release, and during an ex-offender's long-term transition to the community.

Other DOJ Grant Programs. DOJ maintains formula grant programs outlined below that provide assistance to states or local units of government according to legislatively mandated formulas; this funding can be used for offender reentry purposes at the state or local unit of government's discretion. In addition to these programs, the Edward Byrne Justice Assistance Grant program can also be used by states to support offender reentry activities and initiatives [51].

Community Oriented Policing Services (COPS) [52]. The COPS program does not expressly authorize funding for offender reentry purposes [53]; nevertheless, under its broad community policing mandate, OJP has used this grant program on occasion to fund pilot offender reentry programs. The most recent of these was the Value-Based Reentry Initiative (VBRI). As part of this initiative, mentors were chosen from faith-based and community organizations to serve as liaisons between the released offender and the resources and services available in the community, including housing, employment, and health services. Five local organizations participated in the program in Missouri, Michigan, California, Washington DC, and Massachusetts. Funding for the VBRI program expired in FY2005 [54].

The Weed and Seed Program [55]. The Weed and Seed program can also provide funding for state offender reentry programs. According to DOJ, the Weed and Seed program focuses on a two-pronged approach. On the one hand, local law enforcement agencies and prosecutors work together to "weed out" criminals who participate in violent crime and drug abuse. On the other hand, the program seeks to "seed" the community with services, encompassing prevention, intervention, treatment, and neighborhood revitalization. Offender reentry programs can fall under both of these parameters because funding can be used to provide supervision for ex- offenders in the community, as well as to develop support services. In addition to participating in the PRI program, Weed and Seed is currently collaborating with the Corporation for National and Community Service and the Local Initiatives Support Corporation to create volunteer-driven offender reentry initiatives in communities [56].

The Violent Offender Incarceration/Truth in Sentencing Program. Though the main focus of this program was to build or expand correctional facilities to increase the number of convicted violent offenders that can be housed, up to 10% of the award to any given facility could have been used to pay for the cost of offender drug testing and intervention programs for incarcerated offenders, as well as post- release supervision, including funding facilities for transitional housing that allow offenders to be monitored electronically as they reintegrate into their neighborhoods [57]. This program has not received funding since FY200158 and has been unauthorized since FY2000 [59].

Juvenile Justice Grant Programs [60]. The Office of Juvenile Justice and Delinquency Prevention (OJJDP) administers a number of grants that can be used by states and units of local government to provide aftercare services (i.e., offender reentry programs) for juvenile delinquents who are returning to their communities from residential placement (i.e., prison). These programs include the State Formula Grant program, which states can use to fund a variety of programs, including aftercare programs; the State Challenge Grant program, which is a discretionary grant program used to fund innovative approaches to juvenile justice (including the provision of aftercare services); and the Juvenile Mentoring Program, which connects juveniles returning from placement with mentors.

The National Institute of Corrections (NIC). Within the Federal Bureau of Prisons, NIC provides assistance for state and local corrections agencies. NIC provides training, technical assistance, and information services to these agencies, and assists with policy and program development. NIC's offender reentry-related support typically covers programs focused on preparing offenders for offender reentry while they are incarcerated. Specifically, the Office of Correctional Job Training and Placement works to advance the employability of offenders and ex-offenders [61].

Offender Reentry Programs at Other Federal Agencies

As previously mentioned, many federal departments provide funding through a wide array of programs and block grants, which can be used by states for offender reentry. The following list is not meant to be an exhaustive one, but it does capture many programs run by other departments that can be used to support state offender reentry initiatives.

The Department of Labor (DOL). The Workforce Investment Act62 (WIA) of 1998 (P.L.105-220) authorized a nationwide system of workforce development programs, America's Workforce Network, that provides information and services to connect youths and adults with employers [63]. These programs, which can be used by ex-offenders, provide services such as skills-training and job-placement. DOL also instituted a Young Offender Reentry Demonstration Grant Program, which provides funds to communities for offender reentry programs for offenders aged 14 to 21 who are already in the criminal justice system or are considered high-risk. This program focuses on job-training, education, substance-abuse treatment, mental health care, housing assistance, and family support services.

In addition, DOL maintains two programs that provide incentives for companies to hire ex-offenders. The Work Opportunity Tax Credits program [64] provides up to $2,400 in tax credits to companies for every former offender they hire [65], and the Federal Bonding Program [66] allows companies who cannot obtain bonding or insurance from their own providers to bond ex-offenders for up to $25,000 for up to six months [67].

The Department of Education (DOE). Numerous DOE programs can be used by states to help fund or provide technical support for offender reentry programs that focus on education. The Office of Vocational and Adult Education provides several different programs for offender reentry. The Lifeskills for State and Local Inmates Program provides funding for demonstration projects to reduce recidivism through educational services before inmates are discharged into the community [68]. The Grants to States for Workplace and Community Transition Training for Incarcerated Youth Offenders funds postsecondary education and vocational training to people under the age of 25 from five years before their release to one year post-release [69]. Title II of the Workforce Investment Act, Adult Education and Family Literacy, also authorized funding to be appropriated for basic skills instruction; up to 10% of the funds can be used for institutionalized offenders or for ex-offenders in community programs. In addition, the Perkins State Grant Program allows states to use up to 1% of their funds to serve offenders in institutions [70].

The Department of Housing and Urban Development (HUD). HUD funds a variety of programs that help states and local governments to support housing programs. The Community Development Block Grant Program aims to assist states develop viable urban communities. Funds are allocated by formula to the states, and communities and grantees have significant discretion concerning how to allocate their federal funding — including using some funds to provide housing for exoffenders [71].

The Department of Health and Human Services (DHHS). DHHS provides funding for a multitude of programs that can be used to help offender reentry programs through the Substance Abuse and Mental Health Services Agency [72] (SAMHSA) and the Office of Community Services. These programs include the Recovery Community Support Program, which targets people and families recovering from drug abuse and addiction, and several block grant programs. SAMHSA also funds a program that specifically targets offender reentry known as the Young Offender Reentry Program (YORP). The YORP provides funding for state, tribal, and local governments, as well as community based non-profit organizations, to expand substance abuse treatment and supervision programs for juvenile and young adult offenders re-entering the community [73]. Funds for DHHS programs may be used to provide substance abuse or mental health services for offenders on parole or probation. However, DHHS funds may not used to provide services to incarcerated offenders [74].

LEGISLATION IN THE 110TH CONGRESS

A number of bills introduced in the 110th Congress touch on the issue of offender reentry. The only comprehensive offender reentry bills to have seen action thus far in the 110th Congress are H.R. 1593 and S. 1060, commonly known as the Second Chance Act. H.R. 1593 was reported out of the House Committee on the Judiciary on May 9, 2007, and was passed under a motion to suspend the rules by the House on November 13, 2007, by a vote of 347 to 62. S. 1060 was ordered to be reported out of the Senate Committee on the Judiciary on August 2, 2007, but was never actually reported [75]. Instead, the Senate reported H.R. 1593 out of the Senate Committee on the Judiciary by unanimous consent on March 11, 2008; H.R. 1593 was passed by the Senate by unanimous consent on the same day. The President signed the Second Chance Act (P.L. 110-199) into law on April 9, 2008. The following section provides an overview of the bills touching on the issue of offender reentry in the 110th Congress; for a section-by-section analysis of the Second Chance Act, please refer to Appendix A.

The Second Chance Act

A bill called The Second Chance Act has been introduced in each Congress since 2000. While these bills have differed from Congress to Congress, they would all have reformed the offender reentry process. In the 110th Congress, four separate bills have been introduced that include similar language. Two of them, H.R. 1593 and S. 1060, have seen action of some sort. As previously noted, H.R. 1593 was enacted as P.L. 110-199 on April 9. 2008. The other two are S. 2237, a broader crime control bill that includes a section called the Enhanced Second Chance Act, and H.R. 623. Following is a brief discussion of each of these bills.

P.L. 110-199 expands the current offender reentry grant program at DOJ, replacing the four purpose areas currently eligible for funding with new purpose areas spanning every phase of the offender reentry process [76]. Applicants for these grants would be subjected to a number of requirements, including submitting a reentry strategic plan with their application, describing the long-term strategy, and providing a detailed implementation schedule, among other things. The Act requires that states and localities match 50% of the federal funds provided; up to half of this state match (or 25% of the overall total funding) can be composed of in-kind contributions. The Act also directs the Bureau of Prisons (BOP) to modify various components of its offender reentry planning process for federal ex-offenders, establishes a prisoner reentry program at BOP, and endows the agency with new authorities.

The Act also creates some new demonstration grant programs, including

- grants for state and local reentry courts;
- grants for drug treatment diversion programs;
- grants to expand substance-abuse programs for prisoners and ex-offenders; and
- grants to expand the use of career training programs and mentoring programs.

While the Act authorizes a number of new pilot programs and expands the current offender reentry grant program at DOJ, it is important to note here that all of these authorizations are subject to the availability of appropriations. If funding is not appropriated for these programs in FY2009, they will probably not go into effect.

S. 1060 includes language that is largely similar to that found P.L. 110-199; however, S. 1060 included some grant programs that were not included in the Act, such as grants to study the use of drug treatment to reduce illegal drug demand and grants to ensure the availability of pharmacological drug treatment services in prison.

S. 2237, the Crime Control and Prevention Act of 2007, includes Section III, the Enhanced Second Chance Act of 2007. In a number of respects, Section III of S. 2237 is similar to H.R. 1593 and S. 1060. S. 2237 would replace the current offender reentry grant program's four purpose areas with 27 new purpose areas spanning every phase of the reentry process; these purpose areas and the requirements to be eligible for funding are broadly similar to those found in H.R. 1593 and S. 1060. S. 2237 would also direct the Bureau of Prisons (BOP) to establish pre-release planning procedures for ex-offenders, but unlike H.R. 1593 and S. 1060, the bill does not create a new offender reentry program for federal prisoners or provide new authorities to BOP. S. 2237 would create three new grant programs:

- grants to study the effects of revoking an ex-offender's parole,
- grants to community based organizations to provide mentoring and other transitional services to ex-offenders, and
- grants to establish group homes for recovering substance abusers.

Of these three new grant programs, only the group home grant program differs from those that would be established by H.R. 1593 and S. 1060. However, a number of grant programs that are included in H.R. 1593 and S. 1060 are not in S. 2237.

In addition, S. 990 and H.R. 1692, the Fighting Gangs and Empowering Youth Act of 2007, include language similar to that found in H.R. 1593, S. 1060, and S. 2237 that would expand the current offender reentry grant program for ex-offenders and establish a National Adult and Juvenile Offender Reentry Resource Center.

H.R. 623, the Second Chance for Ex-Offenders Act of 2007, has been introduced in each Congress since the 106th Congress. The bill would allow non-violent offenders (defined as offenders who did not use weapons or violence in the course of committing their crimes) to petition to have their criminal records expunged. Eligibility would be restricted to individuals without prior convictions, and petitioners would have to remain free from substance dependency for a minimum of one year and complete at least a year of community service. Once a record is expunged, DOJ would be allowed to disclose the name of the offender and the agency that has custody over the record (but not information concerning the offense) only in certain cases, including criminal investigations, gun applications, and government employment applications. Expunged records would be restored if the individual was convicted for a new crime.

Other Offender Reentry-Related Legislation

S. 456, the Gang Abatement and Prevention Act, was passed by the Senate on September 21, 2007. The bill includes a provision (§ 302) that would establish a Gang Prevention Grant program administered by the Office of Justice Programs at DOJ. Among other purposes, this grant could be used to fund reintegration strategies for the reentry of gang-members into the community. The bill would also create a National Gang Research, Evaluation, and Policy Institute that would be charged, among other things, with facilitating the implementation of data-driven reentry programs for gang-offenders. Similar offender reentry-related language exists in H.R. 3547, the Gang Prevention, Intervention, and Suppression Act.

H.R. 3467, the Second Chance for America's Veterans Act, would direct the Secretary for Veterans Affairs to create a workforce offender reentry grant program for incarcerated veterans. The program would be established in at least 24 locations equitably distributed across the United States, and at least one of these locations would be in a penal institution administered by the Bureau of Prisons. The program would include referral and counseling services in order to assist incarcerated veterans with job training and placement, housing, health care, and other benefits. Grant funding for these purposes would be made available to state agencies, non-profit organizations, and state and local workforce investment boards, and each program funded by this grant would be directed to provide a detailed outcomes report, including recidivism data, to the Secretary of Veterans Affairs. The bill would authorize appropriations of $15 million each year from FY2008 through FY20 11.

H.R. 3409, the Place to Call Home Act, would create a Youth Offender Reentry Grant program. Under this program, the Attorney General would be directed to create a program that would identify incarcerated young adults who would be eligible for release prior to their 25th birthday and provide targeted offender reentry services to these individuals. Pre-release services to be provided would include training in daily living skills, training in parenting skills, training in budgeting and financial management skills, substance abuse prevention, mental health counseling, and preventive health activities. The AG would also be directed to provide any further assistance needed at the pre- and post-release stages to connect offenders with employment, housing, mentors, and post-secondary education. To be eligible for funding, states would be required to submit a plan describing how they plan to meet the program's goals, how funding would be used for both pre- and post-release planning and services, and how funding would be distributed among a diverse range of qualified non-profit and private organizations. States would also be required to make a series of certifications, including, among other things, that not more than 30% of the funds allotted to the state would be used for post-release room and board for eligible ex-offenders, and that public and private organizations have been consulted in developing the plan and given at least 30 days to submit comments on the plan. Funding would be distributed to states based in part on the ratio of the number of individuals in that state between the ages of 13 and 25 compared with the national average. States would be required to collaborate with DOJ in establishing evaluation procedures and data-driven outcome measures; 1.5% of the overall funding for this program would be used by the AG to fund evaluations of the state programs. The bill would authorize $200 million for this program.

S. 1907 and H.R. 3187, the Meth Mouth Correctional Costs and Reentry Support Acts, would establish a grant program to fund programs that would identify, eliminate, and report on the degree to which poor dental health undermines an exoffender's transition to the community. Funding could be used, among other things, to provide dental treatment programs at correctional facilities, promoting oral hygiene among inmates, and assessing the oral condition of inmates at their release. S. 1907 would authorize annual appropriations of $100 thousand each year from FY2009 through FY20 11; H.R. 3187 would authorize $5 million each year over the same time period.

Current Legislative Issues

There are a number of oversight issues relating to the administration of federal offender reentry grant funding that may be of concern to Congress. Following is a brief discussion of selected issues, including the adequacy of the federal government's existing offender reentry grant programs, the lack of coordination between different federal agencies concerning offender reentry, and the lack of current recidivism statistics for ex-offenders.

Adequacy of Existing Offender Reentry Programs

This report has demonstrated the breadth of funding opportunities available in the federal government for offender reentry purposes. As previously discussed, funding that can be used to support offender reentry programs exists in grant programs administered by the Departments of Justice, Labor, Education, Housing and Urban Development, and Health and Human Services. Among the number of federal grant programs that include purpose areas that can be used to fund offender reentry, a handful of programs government-wide were identified that are specifically tailored to offenders for reentry purposes: the Prisoner Reentry Initiative at the Departments of Justice and Labor, the Grants to States for Workplace and Community Transition Training for Incarcerated Youth Offenders and the Lifeskills for State and Local Inmates Program within the Department of Education, and the Young Offender Reentry Program within the Department Health and Human Services.

The comparative lack of targeted offender reentry grant funding may be of issue for Congress because of the apparent need for a wide range of services for offenders both pre- and post-release. According to a report of the Reentry Policy Council, "[a]lthough approximately three of every four people released from incarceration have a history of substance abuse, only 10 percent in state prison and three percent in local jails receive formal treatment prior to release. Just one-third (35 percent) of those released from prison participated in educational programs while incarcerated; even fewer (27 percent) took part in vocational training" [77]. A potential issue for Congress may include whether the current grant programs within the federal government can adequately support state and local correctional systems as they confront the wide array of services that ex-offenders require to successfully transition back to the community. If federal programs are seen as adequate, then no action by Congress may be necessary. Otherwise, policy options could include expanding the purpose areas of existing grant programs that are being funded, either to broaden the types of offender reentry programs that could be funded or to add such programs to grant programs that do not currently include offender reentry among their purpose areas. Another policy option could include creating new grant programs specifically tailored to specific kinds of offender reentry programs, such as housing assistance, drug treatment, or job training programs, among others.

Lack of Current Federal Recidivism Statistics

As previously noted, the only national-level recidivism statistics concerning the reentry of prisoners into the community are more than a decade old. These studies showed that over two-thirds of ex-offenders had come into contact with the legal system, either through a new arrest, a violation of the terms of their release, or a new conviction, within three years of their release. However, there are no current national-level recidivism statistics, and the Bureau of Justice Statistics does not currently have plans to update their recidivism study because of funding constraints [78]. While a number of states have conducted studies of their prisoners' recidivism, the lack of national-level statistics poses a challenge for policy makers as they consider the issue of offender reentry. Without a current, national-level analysis of which ex- offenders are more likely to recidivate, it is difficult to target funding to offender reentry programs that address the at-risk population. Indeed, much of the offender reentry literature being published today continues to cite the Bureau of Justice Statistics study from the mid-1990s when referring to recidivism. A potential issue of interest for Congress may include whether a new, national level recidivism study is needed to better understand the current trends in recidivism and to better target federal funding to the ex-offenders that are most likely to re-offend. Policy options could include providing funding to the Bureau of Justice Assistance to update their 1994 study or to undertake a new study, or funding an educational institution or nonprofit entity to undertake a national-level recidivism study.

Focus on Recidivism

While few would argue that recidivism is the most important measure of an offender reentry program's impact, there is a growing consensus within the offender reentry field that other outcome measures need to be considered when determining whether a program has been effective [79]. Many practitioners believe that an individual's reintegration into the community should be measured by a number of indicators concerning their attachment to social networks, and not just by whether they come into contact with the criminal justice system again. Possible measures of reintegration can include whether an ex-offender has found and maintained a job; whether the ex-offender has reconnected with his family and, if he has children, whether he is supporting them; whether the ex-offender has become involved in his community through participation in church events, neighborhood organizations, and support groups; and whether the ex-offender has attained sobriety or is participating in a treatment program. A potential issue for Congress could include whether these alternate measures of an offender reentry program's effectiveness in fostering reintegration within the community should be considered when deciding how best to allocate grant funding and other government resources. A related issue could be whether reporting on these alternate outcome measures should be required of programs receiving federal grant funding.

Coordination between Federal Agencies

There are a number of entities that bring together offender reentry professionals from state and local governments, non-profit organizations, and academic institutions, including the Reentry Policy Council founded by the Council of State Governments and the Reentry Roundtable hosted by the Urban Institute. Both of these organizations attempt to bolster information sharing about best-practices and funding opportunities and coordination between the various state and local agencies and stake-holders within the offender reentry field. However, the extent to which the various federal agencies with grant programs that can be used for offender reentry purposes coordinate their efforts is currently unclear.

While the Serious and Violent Offender Reentry Initiative, as previously noted, reportedly brought together stakeholders from the Departments of Justice, Labor, Education, and Health and Human Services, that pilot program ended in FY2005 and is currently being evaluated. Over the last two years, DOJ notes that it has coordinated the Prisoner Reentry Initiative with the Department of Labor [80]. Despite the collaborations noted above, it is unclear to what extent these various departments have been coordinating the reentry funding available through their various other grant programs. This raises a potential issue concerning the extent to which duplication of resources is currently occurring across the federal government. A number of the grant programs identified above share purpose areas or can be used to fund similar activities. This could create a certain measure of confusion among state and local entities applying for offender reentry grant funding. There is currently no federal entity currently legislatively charged with coordinating federal offender reentry programs and services across the federal government. A potential issue for Congress could include whether some form of coordinating council or federal offender reentry clearinghouse should be created to provide supervision and oversight to the federal government's offender reentry efforts.

Evaluations of Offender Reentry Programs

As previously noted, there is a comparative lack of scientifically rigorous evaluations of offender reentry programs. The "what works" literature review cited earlier was able to identify only 32 evaluations undertaken over a 30-year span that met their selection criteria; of these, only 2 were randomized control trials. The lack of rigorous evaluations of offender reentry programs makes it difficult for policy makers at every level of government to make informed decisions concerning what programs to fund and what initiatives to support. This may be of issue to Congress during both the appropriations and authorization processes. During the appropriations process, Congress faces decisions about what kinds of grant programs should be funded that are likely to be complicated by the lack of available data concerning what kinds of programs are effective. During the authorization process, as Congress considers whether to modify existing grant programs or create new grant programs, the lack of evidence makes ensuring that effective programs are being created more challenging. Potential issues for Congress to consider could thus include whether more evaluations should be funded through the federal grant process and whether scientific evaluations should be required of existing programs.

Appropriations for the Second Chance Act

The Second Chance Act expanded DOJ's current offender reentry grant program and authorized a number of targeted pilot programs. However, because the Act was enacted in April of 2008, these programs were enacted too late to be included in the President's budget request for FY2009. Indeed, as previously noted, the President's FY2009 request proposes consolidating the DOJ offender reentry grant program into a larger discretionary grant program. Whether funding is to be included in the FY2009 appropriation for the offender reentry programs and activities within DOJ that were authorized by the Second Chance Act will likely be an issue that Congress considers as the FY2009 appropriations bills are debated.

CONCLUSION

This report has shown that over the past two and a half decades, the prison population and the number of ex-offenders being released into the community have been increasing. The increasing number of ex-offenders entering the community has put pressure on public policy makers to provide treatments and services that will smooth the reintegration process while reducing recidivism. When deciding what programs to fund, policy makers often focus on reducing recidivism. The focus on reducing recidivism, however, is complicated by the fact that there are different definitions of recidivism. For example, the last major national-level study showed that two-thirds of ex-offenders came into contact with the legal system and that about half were back in prison within three years of their release. However, only a quarter of the ex-offenders ended up in prison for having committed new crimes; another quarter were back in prison for technical violations of their release (such as failing a drug test). Whether technical violations should be considered a measure of recidivism or whether recidivism should be confined to the commission of new crimes has engendered much debate within the criminal justice field.

While the emphasis on reducing recidivism is important, programs should also be evaluated based on other outcome measures such as their ability to connect ex- offenders with jobs, services, and institutions in their communities. The best available research has shown that there are a number of services that can help ex- offenders reconnect with their communities and lower recidivism, including programs focusing on providing vocational training, substance abuse prevention, mental health services, and alternative housing. The most successful programs focus on high-risk offenders, are intensive in nature, begin during institutional placement, and take place mostly in the community. However, a relative lack of scientifically rigorous research has made it difficult to draw definitive conclusions about which programs are most effective.

As Congress debates this issue, a number of policy issues may be considered, including whether the current federal grant programs are adequate or whether new programs should be created, whether there is a need for more current national-level recidivism data, whether enough coordination of the many programs that may be used to help ex-offenders is occurring within the federal government, whether more evaluations of offender reentry programs are needed, and whether funding will be appropriated for the programs and activities that were authorized by the Second Chance Act.

Appendix A: Section-by-Section Comparison of the Second Chance Act Amendments to Current Offender Reentry Grant Program

The Second Chance Act, P.L. 110-199, was passed by the House on November 13, 2007, and by the Senate on March 11, 2008. The Act was signed into law on April 9, 2008. Following is a section-by-section analysis of the Act's provisions.

Amendments to Current Offender Reentry Grant Program (§ 101)

The Second Chance Act would reauthorize and expand the adult and juvenile offender state and local offender reentry demonstration projects codified at 42 U.S .C. 3797w(b-c). The Act would replace the four current purpose areas eligible for funding with seven broad purpose areas:

- educational, literacy, vocational, and job placement services;
- substance abuse treatment and services, including programs that start in placement and continue through the community;
- programs that provide comprehensive supervision and offer services in the community, including programs that provide housing assistance and mental and physical health services;
- programs that focus on family integration during and after placement for both offenders and their families;
- mentoring programs that start in placement and continue into the community;
- programs that provide victim-appropriate services, including those that promote the timely payment of restitution by offenders and those that offer services (such as security or counseling) to victims when offenders are released; and
- programs that protect communities from dangerous offenders, including developing and implementing the use of risk assessment tools to determine when offenders should be released from prison.

Applicants for these grants would be subjected to a number of requirements, including submitting a reentry strategic plan with their application, describing the long-term strategy, providing a detailed implementation schedule, identifying the local government's role in the plan, and describing the "evidence based methodology and outcome measures" that would be used to evaluate the programs and "provide valid measures" of the program's impact.

The Act would allow the Attorney General (AG) to make grants for these programs if the applications received meet the following conditions:

- they are explicitly supported by the chief executive of the unit of government applying for the funding;
- they extensively discuss the role that the various law enforcement entities involved in the reentry process will have in the program;

- they provide extensive evidence of collaboration among the state and local health, housing, child welfare, education, substance abuse,
- they provide a plan for analyzing any statutory, regulatory, or other hurdles that may exist to reintegrating offenders into the community; and
- they include a reentry taskforce as described below to carry out the activities funded under the grant.

The Act requires applicants to develop a comprehensive strategic reentry plan that contains measurable five-year performance outcomes, with the goal of reducing recidivism by 50% over this period. As a condition of funding, applicants are also required to create offender reentry taskforces that would integrate the prime offender reentry stake-holders in their communities in order to pool resources, facilitate data- collection, and reduce recidivism. Grantees are also required to submit annual reports to DOJ that identify the specific progress made toward achieving their strategic performance outcomes, and may be eligible for future grants if they demonstrate adequate progress towards reducing recidivism by 10% over a two-year period.

In awarding grants under this program, the AG is directed to prioritize applications that

- focus on geographic areas with a disproportionate population of ex-offenders;
- include input from non-profit organizations, consultation with victims and ex-offenders, and coordinate with families;
- demonstrate effective case management in order to provide comprehensive and continuous services during reentry;
- review the adjudications process for parole violations in the applicant's criminal justice system;
- provide for an independent evaluation of the program, including, to the extent practicable, the use of random assignment; and
- target high risk offenders through the use of validated assessment tools.

Additionally, the Act establishes a National Adult and Juvenile Offender Reentry Resource Center by authorizing the AG to make a grant available to an eligible organization. The selected organization are directed to provide education, training, and technical assistance to states and other governments in order to collect and disseminate data and best practices in offender reentry, including the use of evaluation tools and other measures to assess and document performance.

Up to 4% of the authorized level of funding can be used to establish and run this center.

The Act authorizes $55 million in both FY2009 and FY20010 for these programs and limits funding for technical assistance and training to between 2% and 3% of the overall total appropriated. The total federal share of funding for these grants is limited to 50%; however, up to 50% of the state and local matching funds (i.e., 25% of the overall grant) could be fulfilled through in-kind contributions of goods or services.

Improvement of the Residential Substance Abuse Treatment for State Offenders Program (§102)

This provision requires states receiving grants under the residential substance abuse treatment program (42 U.S.C. 3796ff) to ensure that individuals participating in these programs receive aftercare services, including a full continuum of support services. The Act defines residential substance abuse treatment programs as a course of comprehensive individual and group substance abuse services lasting at least six months in residential treatment facilities that are set apart from the general population of a prison or jail. The Act also requires the AG to study the use and effectiveness of the funds used to provide the required aftercare services.

Definition of Violent Offender for Drug Court Program (§103)

The Act modifies the government's current drug court grant program, restricting the current definition of "violent offender" to individuals charged with or convicted for certain offenses that are punishable by a sentence of longer than one year (prior there was no minimum sentence length) [81]. The Act requires all grantees under this program to adhere to this definition of "violent offender" within three years of the enactment of the act (i.e., April 9, 2011), and requires the secretary to publish regulations to this effect within 90 days of enactment. Any drug court not adhering to this definition by April 9, 2011, would see their grant allocations reduced.

New Offender Reentry Grant Programs

Subtitle B creates a number of new targeted grant programs within the Department of Justice (DOJ) relating to the reintegration of offenders into the community.

State and Local Reentry Courts (§111)

This provision creates a new grant program within DOJ to fund reentry courts. Subject to the availability of appropriations, grants up to $500,000 are made available for state and local adult and juvenile court systems in order to establish and maintain reentry courts. These courts will be tasked with monitoring juvenile and adult offenders reentering into the community and providing them with a coordinated and comprehensive array of services, including housing assistance, education, job training, health services, and substance abuse treatment. In order to be eligible for funding, applicants have to demonstrate the need for their program; create a long-term strategy and detailed implementation plan; identify the government and community entities that would be coordinated by the project; and describe the methodology and outcome measures that would be used to evaluate the program. Additionally, applicants are required to submit annual reports to DOJ including a summary of the activities carried out with the grant and an assessment of whether these activities are meeting the needs identified in the grant application. The Act authorizes $10 million for this program in FY2009 and FY20 10. The total federal share of funding for these grants is limited to 50%; however, up to 50% of the state and local matching funds (i.e., 25% of the overall grant) could be fulfilled through in-kind contributions of goods or services.

Drug Treatment Alternative to Prison Programs (§ 112)

This provision creates a new grant program for state and local prosecutors to fund the development, implementation, and expansion of drug treatment programs that are alternatives to imprisonment. The programs require eligible offenders, after having received the consent of the prosecutor, to participate in comprehensive drug treatment programs in lieu of imprisonment. Criminal charges would be dismissed upon completion of the program. Offenders failing to successfully complete their treatment programs would serve their original sentence. In order to be eligible for these programs, the offender in question could not have had any prior felony use of force convictions or have been charged with or convicted of an offense involving a firearm, a dangerous weapon, or the use of force against another individual. The Act authorizes $10 million for this program in FY2009 and FY20 10. The total federal share of funding for these grants is limited to 50%; however, up to 50% of the state and local matching funds (i.e., 25% of the overall grant) could be fulfilled through in-kind contributions of goods or services.

Family Substance Abuse Treatment Alternatives to Incarceration Grants (§113)

This provision creates a new grant program to develop, implement, and expand the use of family-based substance abuse treatment programs as alternatives to incarceration for non-violent parent drug offenders. Among other things, the treatment is required to be clinically appropriate, comprehensive, and long-term and would be provided in a residential setting rather than an outpatient or a hospital setting. The program is required to include the implementation of graduated sanctions applied on the basis of the offender's accountability throughout the course of the program and the development of reentry plans for offenders. Offenders failing to complete the program are required to complete the sentence for the underlying crime involved. Grantees are required to submit annual reports to DOJ detailing the effectiveness of their programs using evidence-based data. Prison-based programs are required to locate their programs in an area separate from the general population, to create and support treatment plans for incarcerated parents, and to ensure continuity of care if participating offenders are transferred to a different facility. The Act authorizes $10 million in FY2009 and in FY2010 for these grants; not less than 5% of this total is to be allocated to Indian Tribes.

Grants to Evaluate and Improve Educational Methods at Prisons, Jails, and Juvenile Facilities (§114)

This program authorizes the AG, subject to the availability of appropriations, to make grants to evaluate, identify, and improve programs that focus on providing educational and vocational programs for offenders by identifying and implementing best practices. Grantees are required to submit reports within 90 days of the last day of the final fiscal year of a grant detailing the progress that they have made. The Act authorizes appropriations of $5 million for this program in FY2009 and FY20 10.

Technology Careers Training Demonstration Grants

The Act authorizes the AG to make grants to states, units of local governments, territories, and Indian Tribes to provide technology career training for prisoners. Grants may be awarded for programs that establish technology careers training programs for offenders during the three-year period prior to their release. Access to the Internet during the program will be restricted to ensure public safety. Grantees must submit a report to DOJ describing and assessing the program each fiscal year. The Act authorizes $10 million for this program in FY2009 and FY20 10.

New Drug-Treatment and Mentoring Grant Programs

Title II of P.L. 110-199 authorizes a series of new grant programms for drug-treatment and mentoring purposes. Subtitle A (§201) focuses on drug treatment programs, Subtitles B and C (§§21 1-2 14) focus on training and mentoring programs, and Subtitle C (§231) would create a federal offender reentry program at the Bureau of Prisons.

Offender Reentry Substance Abuse and Criminal Justice Collaboration Program (§201)

The Act authorizes the AG to make grants to states, units of local governments, territories, and Indian Tribes in order to improve drug treatment programs in prisons and reduce the use of alcohol and other drugs by long-term abusers under correctional supervision. Grants may be used to continue or improve existing drug treatment programs, develop and implement programs for long-term substance abusers, provide addiction recovery support services, and establish pharmacological drug treatment services as part of any drug treatment program offered to prisoners [82]. Grant applicants are required to identify the entities that will be involved in providing the treatment, certify that this treatment has been developed in consultation with the Single State Authority for Substance Abuse [83], certify that the treatment will be clinically appropriate and will provide comprehensive treatment, and describe how evidence-based strategies have been incorporated into the program, including the collection and analysis of data. The AG is required to submit a report to Congress detailing best practices relating to substance abuse treatment in prison and comprehensive treatment of long-term substance abusers by September 30, 2009. Another report on the drug treatment programs funded through this grant program is required by September 30, 2010. The Act authorizes appropriations of $15 million for this program in both FY2009 and FY20 10.

Mentoring Grants to Nonprofit Organizations (§211)

This provision would create a new grant program to provide mentoring and other transitional services for offenders being released into the community. Funding could be used for mentoring programs both in placement and during reentry, programs providing transition services during reentry, and programs providing training for "offender and victims issues." Priority would be given to applicants providing for the evaluation of their programs, using randomized control trials to the maximum extent feasible. Applicants would be required to identify and report on specific outcome performance measures related to the overall goal of reducing recidivism. The bills would authorize $15 million in FY2009 and in FY20 10 for these grants.

Responsible Reintegration of Offenders (§212)

The Act authorizes the Secretary of Labor to make grants to non-profit organizations to provide a wide array of mentoring, job training and job placement services, and other comprehensive transitional services. Grants may not be used to provide substance abuse treatment, mental health treatment, or housing services; however, grants can be used to coordinate with other entities providing these services. Applications for the program must identify the specific eligible area that will be served and the need for support in this area and describe the services that will be provided, the partnerships that have been established with the criminal justice system and housing authorities, and how other sources of funding will be leveraged to provide support services. In order to be eligible for funding, programs must be located in urbanized areas or clusters (as determined by the Bureau of the Census) that have a large number of prisoners returning to the community and high recidivism rates (however, no definitions for a large number of returning prisoners or high recidivism rates are provided). To be eligible for the program, offenders would be at least 18 years old, have no prior adult convictions or convictions for violent or sex- related offenses, and have been released from prison no more than 180 days before they begin participating in the grant program [84]. Not more than 15% of the grant may be used to pay for administrative costs. The Act authorizes $20 million in appropriations for the Secretary of Labor to carry out this section in both FY2009 and FY20 10; up to 4% of the appropriation may be used to provide technical assistance.

Bureau of Prisons Policies on Mentoring Contacts (§213)

This provision would direct the Director of the Bureau of Prisons (BOP) at DOJ to adopt and implement a policy by July 9, 2009, to ensure that mentors working with incarcerated offenders are permitted to continue providing their services to the offender after their release from prison. The Director is required to submit a report to Congress concerning this policy's implementation by September 20, 2009.

Bureau of Prisons Policies on Chapel Library Material (§214)

The Director of the BOP is required to discontinue the Standardized Chapel Library project, or any other project that compiles, lists, or restricts prisoner access to materials provided by chapel libraries by May 9, 2008. Exceptions are made for materials that incite, promote, or suggest violence and materials prohibited by law.

Federal Prisoner Reentry Program (§231)

The Act establishes a prisoner reentry program within the BOP. BOP is required to create a federal prisoner reentry strategy that will

- assess each prisoner's skill level at the beginning of their prison term (including academic, vocational, health, cognitive, interpersonal, daily living, and other related skills);
- create a skills development plan for prisoners to be carried out during their term of imprisonment;

- determine program assignments for prisoners based on the needs identified by the assessment;
- give priority to the reentry needs of high-risk populations, including sex-offenders, career criminals, and prisoners with mental health problems;
- coordinate and collaborate with other criminal justice, community- based, and faith-based organizations;
- collect information about a prisoner's family relationships and parental responsibilities; and
- provide incentives for prisoners to participate in skills development programs.

Incentives for prisoners to participate in skills development programs include allowing offenders to spend the maximum amount of time in community confinement facilities. Additionally, BOP is required to assist offenders in obtaining identification prior to their release.

The Act modifies current law to include a number of new duties for the Director of BOP. These new duties include the establishment of prerelease planning procedures for all federal offenders that help prisoners apply for federal and state benefits prior to their release, and the establishment of reentry planning procedures to provide federal offenders with information in a number of reentry-related areas. BOP is required to establish and implement a system that will allow it to quantitatively track progress in responding to the reentry needs of its inmates and to provide an annual report to the House and Senate Committees on the Judiciary concerning its progress. An annual report is also required containing recidivism statistics for federal prisoners, including information concerning the relative recidivism rates of offenders participating in major inmate programs. After the initial report establishes a baseline recidivism rate for BOP ex-offenders, the Act establishes 5- and 10-year goals of 2% and 5% reductions in this rate, respectively.

BOP is further required to ensure that the United States Probation and Pretrial Services System has medical information for inmates scheduled for release in order to create supervision plans that address the medical and mental health care needs of ex-offenders, and to ensure that each prisoner in community confinement has access to medical and mental health care.

In addition to the offender reentry program established above, the Act also establishes two new programs within BOP:

- A pilot program within BOP to determine the effectiveness of allowing certain elderly, non-violent offenders to serve the remainder of their sentences on home detention. In order to be eligible for this program, offenders would have to be 65 years old or older and have never been convicted of a violent or sex-related crime or given a life-sentence, among other things.

- A program to provide satellite tracking of certain high-risk individuals after their release from prison, in conjunction with the use of graduated sanctions, the provision of reentry related services, and the involvement the offender's family, a victim advocate, and the victim. The Act authorizes $5 million for this purpose in FY2009 and in FY20 10.

Offender Reentry Research (§241)

The Act allows, but does not direct, the National Institute of Justice to conduct research into offender reentry. This research may include a study identifying the number and characteristics of children with incarcerated parents and their likelihood of engaging in criminal activity, a study identifying mechanisms to compare recidivism rates between states, and a study on the characteristics of individuals released from prison who do not recidivate.

The Act also allows, but does not direct, the Bureau of Justice Statistics to conduct research on offender reentry. This research may include an analysis of the populations that present unique reentry challenges, studies to determine the characteristics of individuals who return to prison (including which individuals pose the highest risk to the community), annual reports on the profile of the population leaving detention and entering the community, a national recidivism study every three years, and a study of post incarceration supervision (e.g., parole) violations.

Grants to Study Post-Incarceration Supervision Violations (§242)

This provision creates a new grant program to fund state studies aimed at improving data-collection on offenders who have their post-incarceration supervision revoked in order to better identify which individuals pose the greatest risk to the community. In order to receive funding, states have to certify that their program would collect "comprehensive and reliable data" and have to provide this data to the Bureau of Justice Statistics.

Addressing the Needs of Children of Incarcerated Parents (§243)

This provision directs the AG to collect data and develop best practices concerning the communication and coordination between state corrections and child welfare agencies, especially as they relate to the safety and support of children of incarcerated parents. The best practices developed should include policies, procedures, and programs that could be used to safeguard the parent-child bond during incarceration and assist incarcerated parents in planning for the future and well being of their children.

Study of Effectiveness of Depot Naltrexone for Heroin Addiction (§244)

The act authorizes the AG, acting through the National Institute of Justice, to make grants to public and private research entities to evaluate the effectiveness of depot naltrexone for the treatment of heroin addiction. In order to be eligible for funding, research entities must demonstrate that they conduct research in a public or private institution of higher education, that they plan to work with parole or probation officers for offenders under court supervision, and that they will use randomized control trials to evaluate their programs. Grantees are required to submit reports to DOJ describing and assessing the uses of their grant.

Authorization of Appropriations for Research (§245)

The Act authorizes $10 million in both FY2009 and FY20 10 to carry out the research programs authorized by §§241-244.

Clarification of Authority to Place Prisoner in Community Corrections (§251)

This provision would require the Director of the BOP to ensure, to the extent practicable, that prisoners within the federal correctional system spend up to a year at the end of their sentence focusing on their reentry into the community. As part of this practice, BOP would be authorized to transfer offenders to community correctional facilities or to home confinement (for the shorter of the last 10% or six months of their sentence). The provision would also give BOP the discretion to disregard a court's order that an offender serve part of his sentence in a community correctional facility.

Residential Drug Abuse Program in Federal Prisons (§252)

The Act replaces the current definition of a residential drug abuse program with language defining such a program as a course of individual and group activities and treatment lasting at least six months in residential treatment facilities that are set apart from the general prison population. The Act also stipulate that this treatment can include pharmacotherapies that extend beyond the six-month period.

Contracting for Services for Post-Conviction Supervision of Offenders (§253)

This provision would give the Director of the Administrative Office of the United States Courts the authority to enter into contracts with public and private agencies to monitor and provide a wide array of services to offenders in the community to promote their reintegration.

Extension of National Prison Rape Elimination Commission (§261)

The Act extends the authorization for the National Prison Rape Elimination Commission [85] from three years to five years.

References

[1] U.S. Department of Justice, Office of Justice Programs, "Learn About Reentry," available at [http://www.reentry.gov/learn.html]. Hereafter cited as "Learn About Reentry."

[2] U.S. Department of Justice, Bureau of Justice Statistics, "Reentry Trends in the United States: Recidivism," available at [http://www.ojp.usdoj .gov/bj s/reentry/recidivism.htm]. Hereafter cited as "Reentry Trends."

[3] Wilkinson, Reginald A., Director of the Ohio Department of Rehabilitation and Correction, "Offender Reentry: A Storm Overdue," Paper Prepared for Third National Forum on Restorative Justice, March 2002, available at [http://www.drc.state.oh.us/web/ Articles/article98.htm]. Hereafter cited as "A Storm Overdue."

[4] U.S. Department of Justice, Bureau of Justice Statistics, "State Prison Expenditures 2001," NCJ202949, June 2004, available at [http://www.ojp.usdoj .gov/bj s/pub/pdf/spe0 1 .pdf].

[5] Learn About Reentry.

[6] U.S. Government Accountability Office, "Prisoner Release: Trends and Information on Reintegration Programs," GAO-01-483, June 2001, pp. 19-25. Hereafter referred to as "GAO Prisoner Release Report."

[7] A Storm Overdue.

[8] Taxman, Faye et al., "Targeting for Reentry: Matching Needs and Services to Maximize Public Safety," National Criminal Justice Reference Service, March 25, 2002.

[9] GAO Prisoner Release Report, p. 5.

[10] While this is generally the case, jails on occasion can also include individuals sentenced to prison terms lasting less than one year (misdemeanors) and convicted felons in jurisdictions where the prisons are overpopulated.

[11] From a CRS interview with the Bureau of Justice Statistics, May 17, 2007.

[12] Reentry Trends.

[13] CRS analysis of Bureau of Justice Statistics data.

[14] CRS analysis of Bureau of Justice Statistics and Census Data.

[15] United Kingdom Home Office, Research, Development, and Statistics Directorate, "World Prison Population List," available at [http://www.csdp.org/research/r234.pdf].

[16] While some states have a parole system in place, Congress abolished parole at the federal level effective in 1986. However, there is a small percentage of federal offenders who were sentenced prior to 1986 who are still eligible for parole.

[17] A determinate sentence is a fixed sentence, while an indeterminate sentence is typically expressed as a range (i.e., 5 to 10 years). For additional information on sentencing guidelines, please refer to CRS Report RL32766, Federal Sentencing Guidelines: Background, Legal Analysis, and Policy Options, by Lisa Seghetti and Alison Smith.

[18] Year-end populations are calculated on December 31 of each year.

[19] The figure does not include federal parole entries and exits.

[20] U.S. Department of Justice, Bureau of Justice Statistics, *Truth in Sentencing in State Prisons*, NCJ170032, January 1999.

[21] For an expanded discussion of the varying definitions of recidivism, refer to Allen Beck, Recidivism: A Fruit Salad Concept in the Criminal Justice World, Justice Concepts, available at [http://www.justiceconcepts.com/recidivism.pdf].

[22] See Colorado Department of Corrections, Recidivism and Cumulative Return Rates: Calendar Year Releases from 1999 through 2005, available at [http://www.doc.state.co.us/Statistics/pdfs/Recidivism/2007RecidBulletin.pdf].

[23] See Florida Department of Corrections, *Recidivism Report: Inmates Released from Florida Prisons,* May 2001, available at [http://www.dc.state.fl.us/pub/recidivism/200 1/ full.pdf].

[24] Patrick A. Langan and David J. Levin, United States Department of Justice, Bureau of Justice Statistics, *Recidivism of Prisoners Released in 1994*, Report NCJ193427, June 2002. Hereafter referred to as "1994 Recidivism Study."

[25] The states included in the study were Arizona, California, Delaware, Florida, Illinois, Maryland, Michigan, Minnesota, New Jersey, New York, North Carolina, Ohio, Oregon, Texas, and Virginia.

[26] 1994 Recidivism Study, p. 7.

[27] United States Sentencing Commission, *A Comparison of the Federal Sentencing Guidelines Criminal History Category and the U.S. Parole Commission Salient Factor Score.*

[28] For examples of how the CHC system works within the federal sentencing guidelines, please refer to CRS Report RL32846, *How the Federal Sentencing Guidelines Work: Two Examples*, by Charles Doyle.

[29] Joan Petersilla, "What Works in Prisoner Reentry? Reviewing and Questioning the Evidence," *Federal Probation*, vol. 68, no. 2, 2004, pp. 4-8. Hereafter referred to as "Questioning the Evidence."

[30] Drug court programs typically divert nonviolent offenders arrested for drug-related crimes to treatment centers as opposed to prison.

[31] Questioning the Evidence, p. 7.

[32] Richard P. Seiter and Karen R. Kadela, "Prisoner Reentry: What Works, What Does Not, and What Is Promising," *Crime and Delinquency*, vol. 49, no. 3, 2003, pp. 360-388. Hereafter referred to as "Prisoner Reentry: What Works."

[33] Questioning the Evidence, 4-5.

[34] Questioning the Evidence, p. 5.

[35] Prisoner Reentry: What Works, p. 370.

[36] Meta-analyses are a type of systematic review of studies that allow researchers to draw conclusions across a wide range of studies by using statistical methods to derive quantitative results from the analysis of multiple sources of quantitative evidence.

[37] Lawrence W. Sherman, Denise Gottfredson, Doris MacKenzie, John Eck, Peter Reuter, and Shawn Bushway, *Preventing Crime: What Works, What Doesn't, What's Promising,* National Institute of Justice, 1997.

[38] Offender Reentry: What Works.

[39] Offender Reentry: What Works, pp. 370-373.

[40] See, for example, Shawn Bushway and Peter Reuter, "Labor Markets and Crime Risk Factors," in *Preventing Crime: What Works, What Doesn't, What's Promising. A Report to the United States Congress*, the National Institute of Justice, 1997, Chapter 6. Jeremy Travis, *But They All Come Back: Facing the Challenges of Prisoner Reentry,* The Urban Institute Press, 2005.

[41] Prisoner Reentry: What Works, pp. 373-374.

[42] Prisoner Reentry: What Works, p. 374.

[43] Prisoner Reentry: What Works, p. 378. A study's statistical significance is typically interpreted as a level of confidence (usually expressed as a probability, e.g., 95%) that an estimated impact is not merely the result of random variation, indicating that at least some of the measured impact may, with substantial confidence (e.g., 95% confidence), be attributed to the treatment as a cause.

[44] Prisoner Reentry: What Works, pp. 376-379.

[45] For more information about the use of randomized control trials to evaluate government programs, refer to CRS Report RL33301, *Congress and Program Evaluation: An Overview of Randomized Controlled Trials (RCTs) and Related Issues*, by Clinton Brass, Blas Nuñez-Neto, and Erin D. Wiliams.

[46] Questioning the Evidence, p. 7.

[47] Questioning the Evidence, pp. 6-7.

[48] P.L. 107-273, Title II, Division B, § 2421(a). Codified at 42 U.S.C. 3797w.

[49] U.S. Department of Justice, Office of Justice Programs, *2005 Congressional Budget Justifications*, p. 37.

[50] The Urban Institute and RTI International, *National Portrait of the Serious and Violent Offender Reentry Initiative*, available at [http://www.urban.org/UploadedPDF/1000692_SVORINationalPortrait.pdf].

[51] For more information about the Justice Assistance Grant program, please refer to CRS Report RS224 16, *Edward Byrne Memorial Justice Assistance Grant Program: Legislative and Funding History, by Nathan James.*

[52] For more information about the COPS program, please refer to CRS Report RL33308, *Community Oriented Policing Services (COPS): Background, Legislation, and Issues,* by Nathan James.

[53] See 42 U.S.C. 3796dd.

[54] U.S. Department of Justice, "Value-Based Initiative and Value-Based Reentry Initiative," COPS Fact Sheet, April 10, 2006.

[55] For more information about this program, please refer to CRS Report RL33489, *An Overview and Funding History of Select Department of Justice (DOJ) Grant Programs*, by Nathan James.

[56] Office of Justice Programs, Community Capacity Development Office, "Reentry," available at [http://www.ojp.usdoj.gov/ccdo/programs/reentry.html].

[57] See Office of Justice Programs, "Violent Offender Incarceration/Truth-in-Sentencing Incentive Grant Program," available at [http://www.ojp.usdoj .gov/BJA/grant/VOITISpurp.pdf], and U.S. Department of Labor, Employment and Training Administration, "Serious and Violent Offender Reentry Initiative Appendices," available at [http://www.doleta.gov/sga/sga/reentry_app.cfm].

[58] Bureau of Justice Assistance, "Violent Offender Incarceration and Truth-in-Sentencing (VOI/TIS) Incentive Program," available at [http://www.ojp.usdoj .gov/BJA/grant/voitis. html].

[59] See 42 U.S.C. 13701 et seq.

[60] For more information about juvenile justice grant programs, please refer to CRS Report RL33947, Juvenile Justice: Legislative History and Current Legislative Issues, by Blas Nuñez-Neto.

[61] U.S. Department of Labor, Employment and Training Administration, "Serious and Violent Offender Reentry Initiative Appendices," available at [http://www.doleta.gov/sga/sga/ reentry_app.cfm].

[62] U.S. Department of Labor, Employment and Training Administration, "Serious and Violent Offender Reentry Initiative Appendices," available at [http://www.doleta.gov/sga/sga/ reentry_app.cfm].

[63] For more information about the Workforce Investment Act, please refer to CRS Report RL33687, *The Workforce Investment Act (WIA): Program-by-Program Overview and Funding of Title I Training Programs*, by Blake Naughton.

[64] For more information about the Work Opportunity Tax Credits Program, please refer to CRS Report RL30089, *The Work Opportunity Tax Credit (WOTC),* by Linda Levine.

[65] U.S. Department of Labor, Employment and Training Administration, "Work Opportunity Tax Credit" available at [http://www.doleta.gov/ business/ Incentives/opptax/].

[66] For more information about the Federal Bonding Program, please refer to CRS Report RL3 0248, The Employment Service: *The Federal-State Public Labor Exchange System*, by Alison Pasternak and Ann Lordeman.

[67] U.S. Department of Labor, Employment and Training Administration, "Federal Bonding Program," available at [http://www.bonds4jobs.com/ program-background.html].

[68] U.S. Department of Education, "Life Skills for State and Local Prisoners Program," available at [http://www.ed.gov/programs/lifeskills/index.html].

[69] U.S. Department of Education, "Guide to U.S. Department of Education Programs, FY2007," p. 38, available at [http://www.ed.gov/programs/ gtep/gtep.pdf].

[70] U.S. Department of Labor, Employment and Training Administration, "Serious and Violent Offender Reentry Initiative Appendices," available at [http://www.doleta.gov/sga/sga/ reentry_app.cfm].

[71] U.S. Department of Labor, Employment and Training Administration, "Serious and Violent Offender Reentry Initiative Appendices," available at [http://www.doleta.gov/sga/sga/r eentry_app.cfm].

[72] For more information about SAMHSA, please refer to CRS Report RL33997, *Substance Abuse and Mental Health Services Administration (SAMHSA)*: Reauthorization Issues, by Ramya Sundararaman.

[73] Testimony of Senior Policy Advisor to the Administrator Cheri Nolan, Substance Abuse and Mental Health Services Administration, U.S. Department of Health and Human Services, before the Committee on the Judiciary, Subcommittee on Corrections and Rehabilitation, Thursday, September 21, 2006.

[74] U.S. Department of Labor, Employment and Training Administration, "Serious and Violent Offender Reentry Initiative Appendices," available at [http://www.doleta.gov/sga/sga/ reentry_app.cfm].

[75] As of December 11, 2007, the text of S. 1060, as ordered reported, has not been made available.

[76] H.R. 1593 includes 7 broadly written purpose areas, whereas S. 1060 includes 21 more specific purpose areas. Despite this difference, the grant program in both bills would fund the same kinds of activities.

[77] Council of State Governments, Re-Entry Policy Council, *Report of the Re-Entry Policy Council: Charting the Safe and Successful Return of Prisoners to the Community*, January 2005, p. 3.

[78] From a telephone conversation with the Bureau of Justice, August 8, 2007.

[79] See, for example, Jeremy Travis, "In Thinking About 'What Works,' What Works Best?," Margaret Mead Address at the National Conference of the International Community Corrections Association held in Indianapolis, Indiana, on November 10, 2003, Urban Institute Justice Policy Center; James Lynch, "Prisoner Reentry: Beyond Program Evaluation," Criminology and Public Policy, vol. 5, no. 2, May 2006; and Questioning the Evidence.

[80] *Learn About Reentry.*

[81] In order to be considered a "violent offender," an individual has to have committed this crime while in possession of a firearm or dangerous weapon, the crime has to have resulted in the death or serious bodily injury of a person, force had to have been used against someone's person, or the offender had 1 or more prior convictions for a felony crime of violence involving the use or attempted use of force against a person with the intent to cause death or serious bodily harm. See 42 U.S.C. 3797 u-2(a)(1).

[82] Pharmacological drug treatment involves using drugs and medications in the treatment of substance abuse. See Clayton Mosher, Scott Akins, and Chad Smith, "Pharmacological Drug Treatment" Paper presented at the annual meeting of the American Society of Criminology, Royal York, Toronto. 2008-04-21.

[83] States would be required to identify an entity that would be the single State administrative authority responsible for planning, developing, implementing, monitoring, regulating, and evaluating substance abuse services within the State.

[84] Grantees may exempt 10% of their clients from this 180 day requirement.

[85] 42 U.S.C. 15606(d)(3)(A).

In: Military Medical Care ISBN 978-1-60692-575-1
Editor: Linda F. Bernstein et al., pp. 55-152 © 2009 Nova Science Publishers, Inc.

Chapter 2

MASS INCARCERATION IN THE UNITED STATES: AT WHAT COST?*

U.S. Government Printing Office

Thursday, October 4, 2007
Congress of the united states, joint economic committee,
Washington, DC

The Committee met at 10:04 a.m. in room 216 of the Hart Senate Office Building, the Honorable Jim Webb and Vice Chair Carolyn B. Maloney, presiding.

Senators present: Webb, Casey, and Brownback. Representatives present: Maloney, English, Scott, and Hin-chey.

Staff present: Christina Baumgardner, Stephanie Dreyer, Chris Frenze, Nan Gibson, Gretta Goodwin, Rachel Greszler, Colleen Healy, Aaron Kabaker, Israel Klein, Michael Laskawy, Zachary Luck, Robert O'Quinn, Jeff Schlagenhauf, and Robert Weingart.

---

* Excerpted from S. HRG. 110–299, dated October 4, 2007.

OPENING STATEMENT OF HON. JIM WEBB, U.S. SENATOR FROM VIRGINIA

Senator Webb [presiding]. The Committee will come to order. I would like to thank Chairman Schumer for agreeing to hold this important hearing, and for allowing me the opportunity to chair it.

I would also like to thank our witnesses for appearing today and, following my remarks, I would ask Vice Chair Maloney and Senator Brownback to make some opening remarks. We also have Congressman Bobby Scott over from the House side who has worked long and hard on these issues and would like to say a few words. Then if Congressman English would like to say something, we will get an opening statement from him.

Then we will turn this over for up to 8-minute summaries of statements from the panel, and then we will go into questions.

Over the course of the period from the mid-1970s until today, the United States has embarked on one of the largest public policy experiments in our history.

Yet this experiment remains shockingly absent from the public debate. The United States now imprisons a higher percentage of its citizens than any other country in the world.

In the name of getting tough on crime, there are now 2.1 million Americans in Federal, State, and local prisons and jails, more people than the populations of New Mexico, West Virginia, or several other States.

Compared to our democratic advanced-market economy counterparts, the United States has more people in prison by several orders of magnitude. All told, more than 7 million Americans are under some form of corrections supervision, including probation and parole.

America's incarceration rate raises several serious questions. These include: The correlation between mass imprisonment and crime rates; the impact of incarceration on minority communities and women; the economic costs of the prison system; criminal justice policy; and transitioning ex-offenders back into their communities and into productive employment.

Equally important, the prison system today calls into question the effects on our society at a broad level. Winston Churchill noted in 1910, "The mood and temper of the public in regard to the treatment of crime and criminals is one of the most unfailing tests of the civilization of any country."With the world's largest prison population, our prisons test the limits of our democracy and push the boundaries of our moral identity.

The growth in the prison population is only nominally related to crime rates. Just last week, in The Washington Post, the Deputy Director of the Bureau of Justice Statistics stated, and I quote, "The growth in the incarceration rate wasn't really about increased crime but how we choose to respond to crime."The steep increase in the number of people in prison, is driven, according to most experts, by changes in drug policy and tougher sentencing, and not necessarily an increase in crime.

Also, the composition of prison admissions has shifted towards less serious offenses—parole violations and drug offenses. Nearly 6 in 10 persons in State prisons for a drug offense have no history of violence or significant selling activity.

In 2005, four out of five drug arrests were for possession and only one out of five were for sales. Is incarcerating low-level drug offenders working, particularly given recidivism rates?

The racial composition of America's prisons is alarming. Although African Americans constitute 14 percent of regular drug users, they are 37 percent of those arrested for drug offenses and 56 percent of persons in State prisons for drug crimes.

African Americans serve nearly as much time in Federal prisons for drug offenses as Whites do for violent crimes.

A Black male who does not finish high school now has a 60-percent chance of going to jail. One who has finished high school has a 30-percent chance.

We have reached a point where the principal nexus between young African American men in our society is increasingly becoming the criminal justice system, and we are spending enormous amounts of money to maintain this system.

The combined expenditures of local, State, and Federal governments for law enforcement and corrections personnel now total over $200 billion.

Prison construction and operations has become a sought after, if uncertain, tool of economic growth for rural communities.

Are there ways to spend less money, enhance public safety, and make a fairer prison system?

Having such a large prison population also has significant employment and productivity implications. The economic output of prisoners is mostly lost to society while they are in prison. These negative productivity effects continue in many cases after release.

As we have gotten tough on crime, we have given up on rehabilitating offenders. And we have created additional barriers to reentry with invisible punishments. These include: ineligibility for government benefits, such as housing, public assistance, or student loans. It is no longer simply possible to pay one's debt to society.

We all want to keep bad people off our streets. We want to break the back of gangs. We want to cut down on violent behavior. But there is something else going on when we are locking up such a high percentage of our people, marking them at an early age, and, in many cases, eliminating their chances for productive life as full citizens.

It will take years of energy to address these problems, but I am committed to working toward a solution that is both responsive to our needs for law and order and fairer to those ensnared by this system.

I welcome the thoughts of our witnesses today regarding these important topics, and also the beginning of a new national dialogue to address these enormous policy issues.

[The prepared statement of Senator Webb appears in the Submissions for the Record on page 41.]

With that, I would call on Vice Chair Maloney.

Opening Statement of Hon. Carolyn B. Maloney, Vice Chair, U.S. Representative from New York

Vice Chair Maloney. Thank you very much. First of all, I join you in thanking Chairman Schumer for holding this hearing to examine the economic, political, and social costs of incarceration. I also thank Senator Webb for chairing, and all of the panelists and all of my colleagues here today.

The United States has the highest incarceration rates in the world with more than 2 million Americans currently in jails or prisons.

Clearly, imprisonment benefits society and is an important public safety measure, but faced with an unprecedented increase in incarceration we must ask ourselves whether we are striking the right balance between the costs and benefits of imprisonment.

Putting more resources into creating economic opportunities that provide alternatives to crime would pay dividends in reducing crime and incarceration, while also strengthening families and communities.

We all know that, in the long run, crime does not pay, but it sure is costly. The average annual cost of incarceration for one Federal prisoner exceeds \$20,000 a year, far more than the average annual cost of \$3,700 for participating in a youth program for a year; or $6,000 for one of our young people to attend job training; or the $13,000 that we would pay for tuition at public universities.

There is absolutely no question that crime rates have dropped in the United States over the past decade. Researchers agree that the increase in incarceration rates have been driven by tougher sentences for repeat offenders and drug offenders, mandatory minimums, and a more punitive approach to post-release supervision, rather than an increase in crime.

The racial dimension of incarceration is inescapable. Half of our prison population is African American, yet they represent just 13 percent of the population of our country as a whole.

It has become a sad truth that a Black man in his late twenties without a high school diploma is more likely to be in jail than to be working. The effect on Black communities has been devastating.

As noted, Harvard sociologist Orlando Patterson wrote in the New York Times recently: one in three African American males in their thirties now has a prison record. He somberly noted, and I quote, "These numbers and rates are greater than anything achieved at the height of the Jim Crow era," end quote.

Women are typically convicted of nonviolent offenses. Most women who enter the criminal justice system have experienced physical or sexual abuse and many have physical or mental health problems.

These inmates may actually benefit from alternatives to imprisonment such as suspended sentences coupled with extensive counseling. When mothers are incarcerated their children may be placed in foster care or with other family members who then need financial assistance to provide for the children.

Moreover, the removal of a significant family member can affect the healthy development of children. The Catholic Charities Diocese in my district, located in Queens and in Brooklyn, operate a week-long summer camp that provides opportunities for incarcerated mothers to have quality time with their children.

Such programs serve as a means to maintain family bonds and possibly provide a smoother transition and resumption of parental responsibilities upon release.

If this program shows success, it could serve as a model for the Nation. Providing employment and training assistance for ex-offenders, is critical to reducing barriers to employment, and it benefits families and benefits society.

I support the Second Chance Act of 2007, which provides grants for re-entry programs that provide mentoring, academic, and vocational education, employment assistance, and substance abuse treatment for ex-offenders.

I look forward to hearing from our distinguished panelists on how best to protect public safety, while addressing the many costs of imprisonment. I might add, the way that we release men and women from prison, with absolutely no assistance, leads, in many cases, to them becoming second offenders, because they have no place to go, they have no money, and, in many cases, have no help.

So this is an important hearing. I congratulate the Senator for leading us to this moment today. Thank you.

[The prepared statement of Vice Chair Maloney appears in the Submissions for the Record on page 43.]

Senator Webb. I thank the Vice Chair. I have been asked to announce that there is a blue backpack in the back of the room. Has it been claimed? Whoever— OK, thank you. You have helped us move the hearing along without an evacuation of the room.

[Laughter.]

Senator Webb. Senator Brownback, we are very grateful for your coming today, and I know you have done a lot of work in this area. You now have the floor.

STATEMENT OF HON. SAM BROWNBACK, U.S. SENATOR FROM KANSAS

Senator Brownback. Thank you very much, Mr. Chairman. I appreciate you holding this hearing and the comments by Vice Chair Maloney and her thoughts on this, as well.

I have worked on this a lot. I have spent time in prison. I may be the only one in here that has spent a night in Louisiana in a State prison there, and one in my State.

I did not have a record, but I went in and stayed, because I was interested in the programs that were taking place in these places, because the numbers are stark.

They are terrible, and they are quite an indictment of our society. But I was looking for something that worked, and what I found, are some very innovative programs around the country, that particularly target the recidivism rates, which, to me, that is one of the key things we can work on, is getting that recidivism rate down.

Right now, the recidivism rate in the country, is roughly about two-thirds; two-thirds of the people that go into State, local, or Federal prisons, in this country, will go back.

And their family members are five times more likely to go into prison, so it seems like—as somebody raised on a farm, you hoe where the weeds are. This is where our problem is, and let's go in and let's deal in those particular areas.

And that is the targeted focus of the Second Chance Act, a series of grants for innovative programs that will cut recidivism rates in half in 5 years.

And it is eclectic, it says, you know, whatever you have got that is working—great, but if it does not work, we are not going to continue it.

It is measurable, recidivism rates cut in half in 5 years, and I think that is not soft on crime; I think that is smart on crime.

And it is something that we need to do, and it is also humanitarian in recognizing that every person is a beautiful, unique soul, a child of a living god, regardless of whether they are in prison or not.

And it tries to treat the individual as a person. I have had a guy sometime back who said, we get into problems when we look at people as problems and not as people. That includes somebody that has committed a crime, even very difficult and bad crimes.

So I think we have got some things we need to change here, how we look at people in prison, what we do on bringing them out of prison.

I think we have got a good model in the Second Chance Act. It has passed the Judiciary Committee, it is a bipartisan bill. It is ready for floor action, and I know that Chairman Webb is a cosponsor of the bill, as well.

I would hope this would be something that this Congress could get done. I think we can get a signature on it from President Bush, and really target this particular area of this problem.

It does not fix the whole thing, but it does get at a particularly key area. It is something that can work and support these innovative programs.

I look forward to the panelists' presentations, and I particularly appreciate Pat Nolan coming here on short notice. They have worked on these topics a lot, and I hope we can move forward with this topic and get something actually accomplished. Thank you, Mr. Chairman.

[The prepared statement of Senator Brownback appears in the Submissions for the Record on page 44.]

Senator Webb. Thank you very much, Senator Brownback. Congressman Scott, who also has worked many, many years on this, we appreciate you coming over to be part of the hearing this morning, and you may feel free to make a statement.

STATEMENT OF HON. ROBERT C. "BOBBY" SCOTT, U.S. REPRESENTATIVE FROM VIRGINIA

Representative Scott. Thank you, Senator Webb. I want to thank Senator Schumer and Vice Chair Maloney for the opportunity to be with you today as we discuss the very important subject of the costs of mass incarceration we have seen in the United States.

Today, the United States is the world's leading incarcerator, by far, with an average incarceration rate of over seven times the international average.

The average incarceration rate in the rest of the world, is somewhere around 100 per 100,000, and the rate in the United States is over 700 per 100,000. In some inner city communities, the rate goes above 4,000 per 100,000.

Russia has the next closest rate of incarceration, with 611 per hundred thousand, and everybody else is much lower. For example, in India, the world's largest democracy, the rate is 30 per 100,000. In China, the world's largest country, by population, the rate is 118 per 100,000.

We did not get here overnight. I have learned that when it comes to crime policy, we have a choice: You can reduce crime or you can play politics.

And the politics of crime is the get-tough approach, such as more life with parole, mandatory minimum sentences, treating more juveniles as adults. With this approach, no matter how tough we got last year, we get tougher this year.

We have been putting more and more people in jail, and in the last 30 years, we have gone from approximately 300,000 persons incarcerated in the United States in 1970 to over 2 million today. The annual costs have gone up to $65 billion a year.

And the United States has some of the world's most severe punishments for crime, including for juveniles. For more than 2,200 juveniles sentenced in the world to life without parole, all but 12 are in the United States.

Research and analysis, as well as common sense, tells us that no matter how tough you are on people who you prosecute for crimes today, unless you are addressing the reasons they got to the point to commit crimes in the first place, the next wave developing in the system will simply replace those that you take out. And the crime continues.

This is not to say that we should not prosecute crimes, or that imprisonment has no impact. The problem is that you reach a point of diminishing returns, with no appreciable benefit.

In fact, you run the risk of diminishing returns to actually being counterproductive. For example, when you have so many people in a community with criminal records, that the criminal record no longer has a stigma or deterrent effect, you have lost your deterrent effect of the criminal justice system, altogether.

The corollary cost of mass incarceration resulting from the toughon-crime politics unfortunately falls, as we have heard, disproportionately among minorities, particularly Black and Hispanic youth.

The sad reality is that many children born in minority communities today are, from birth, without appropriate intervention, on what is called the cradle-to-prison pipeline.

When you see how simple it is to get them on a cradle-to-college pipeline, it is tragic and much more costly to society, economically and socially, if we do not do so.

There are other costs to consider when crime rates are high, such as the high medical costs associated with gun crimes. One study suggested that actuarial science estimated that the annual cost of gun violence in the United States is approximately $100 billion.

Fortunately, we have a choice. All credible research and evidence shows that a continuum of evidence-based programs for youth identified as being at risk of involvement in delinquent behavior, and those already involved, will not only put kids on an appropriate pipeline towards college, rather than prison, but it will also save more money than it costs.

Washington State did an extensive study that showed that evidence-based prevention and rehabilitation programs, such as drug treatment, reduce crime and save money, when compared to waiting for crimes to be committed and then sending offenders to prison.

Washington State adopted many of the initiatives in that study and, consequently, avoided having to build a new prison as a result There are huge opportunity costs in not doing what the research and evidence tells us will reduce crime.

To illustrate, let's examine the impact in Virginia of the lost opportunities associated with the get-tough crime policy called abolish parole. Rather than invest in proven crime-reduction measures that work, Virginia chose to go down the costly and wasteful path of abolishing parole.

The proponents suggested that even if it worked perfectly, the reduction in violent crime would be a statistically insignificant 3 percent, and even that would be without considering the counterproductive effects of no parole, such as the fact that you cannot hold hardened criminals longer, and the loss of incentive for prisoners to get an education and job training while in prison.

They estimated that the cost of abolishing parole would be $2.2 billion to build new prisons, and about a billion-a-year operating costs.

Now, let's just do a little quick, back-of-the-envelope arithmetic of that kind of budget. There are 11 congressional districts in Virginia, so that is about $200 million for construction and $90 for operations in each congressional district of about 600,000.

So, for a city of 100,000, we are talking $30 million in construction and $15 million in operating. Let's see what you could have done with that.

For $30 million, you could have built ten $3 million Boys and Girls Clubs or family resource centers. With the operating expenses, you could have run those clubs and family resource centers at $600,000 a year, and that would be $6 million.

You could have a thousand summer jobs and that would be another million; a thousand summer camp scholarships at $1,000 and that would be another million; 4,000 after-school programs at $250, another million; 2,000 college scholarships at $2,000, and that is $4 million; services for 200 juveniles at $10,000 a year, $2 million. You could have done all of that, or you could codify a slogan without even knowing if you are reducing crime or even increasing crime.

Of course, we have so many people locked up that we are seeing, a large number returning to the communities, in most cases, no better than when they started out.

This year, we have 650,000 people being released from State and Federal prisons, along with 9 million leaving local jails. The recidivism rate of 67 percent has to be dealt with.

Over one-third of the jailed inmates have physical or mental disabilities, many had drug problems, and with no parole, no good conduct credits, and other self development initiatives being eliminated, we have limited vocational and other developmental programs while in prison.

All of that, along with the disqualifications that result from having a felony record, make it easy to see why the recidivism rate is so high.

One program that has been hugely successful is the Federal Prison Industries, but unfortunately, that program has just been undermined with the provision in the Senate Defense Authorization bill.

The Second Chance Act now pending before Congress will provide a host of evidence-based approaches designed to reduce the high rate of recidivism now occurring; and if we are going to continue to send more and more people to prison with longer and longer sentences, we should do as much as we reasonably can to ensure that when they return from prison, they do not turn around and go back to prison because of new crimes.

The primary reason for doing so is not to benefit the offenders, although it does; the primary reason for doing so is that it better assures that all of us and other members of the public will be less likely to be victims of crime due to recidivism, and we will also save the high costs of law enforcement and incarceration.

Now, Mr. Chairman, I thank you for holding this very important hearing and for inviting me to sit with you today.

[The prepared statement of Representative Robert C. "Bobby"Scott appears in the Submissions for the Record on page 45.]

Senator Webb. Thank you very much, Congressman Scott. Are there any other Committee members who wish to make an opening statement before we go to the witnesses? Senator Casey?

Senator Casey. Mr. Chairman, I want to thank you for calling this hearing, and I want the audience to know, as a first-year Senator, how thrilling it is to be able to call Jim Webb, Mr. Chairman.

[Laughter.]

Senator Webb. There is hope.

[Laughter.]

Senator Casey. And, Chairwoman Maloney, thank you for your work on this issue and so many others.

Vice Chair Maloney. Thank you.

Senator Casey. I do not have a long statement, but I do want to say that the problem that we are here to discuss today and the testimony we will hear from this distinguished panel, as we all know, is both a human tragedy and a fiscal nightmare, and we are well aware of that.

But I think it is important that we do our best today to listen and to learn, and I am honored to be in the presence of so many people who have labored in this vineyard for a long time. We are grateful for the work that is already been done.

But as you can see from this panel, from the Members of Congress who are here, as well as others, that this is a bipartisan challenge. Neither party has a corner on the market, so to speak, of knowledge and wisdom and insight and legislation.

Both parties, I think, are deeply concerned about this. I have to say that one of the reasons that we're in this demographic and fiscal challenge, and why so many lives have been ruined, is that we failed, I think, as a country, and both parties have failed to invest in children in the dawn of their lives.

That's not the whole reason, that is not the only reason we have this problem, but that is a big part of the problem.

I have a bill on pre-kindergarten education and Chairwoman Maloney has similar legislation in the House, and others have worked on this, but I think that today, it is not enough to curse the darkness of that failure to invest.

We could do that all day long, and that is not enough. We have to be concerned about the children and the young adults who did not get the benefit of those investments. We have to deal with them.

We cannot just talk about what should have happened to them; we have got to deal with the challenges in their lives. So, I know that this hearing today will bring light to that darkness, and will further amplify and develop solutions to this problem, so I thank the Chairman, and I am happy to be here today.

Senator Webb. Thank you very much, Senator Casey. Any others? Congressman Hinchey?

Representative Hinchey. Senator Webb, I just want to briefly express my appreciation to you for drawing our attention to this very important issue.

And it really is something that needs to be dealt with. It is another example, I think, of kind of a self-inflicted wound that we have put on our society.

And we have done so until fairly recently. Up until the mid- 1970s, the incarceration rate in the United States, was fairly even with the rest of the world and we were not putting ourselves up front in any way.

But policies changed back then, and over the course of the last 35 years, the number of people that we have locked up in prisons and jails across the country has gone up by more than 700 percent.

So this is an issue that really needs to be dealt with, and it is an issue that we can deal with. This Congress must address it.

It is, in part, I think, an example of how capitalism can be used badly to deal with issues in ways that just make those issues even worse to confront.

So Senator, I deeply appreciate your attention to this, and the opportunity you have given us to learn more about it from this distinguished panel.

And the incentive that, hopefully, this will provide for us to make appropriate corrections.

Senator Webb. Thank you very much. Congressman English, did you wish to make a statement?

Representative English. Let me just say, Mr. Chairman, that I am delighted we are doing this hearing. It is immensely timely.

I will submit my remarks for the record, with the idea that we can hopefully proceed now to our much-awaited testimony from this excellent panel.

Senator Webb. Thank you very much. We do have a very distinguished panel. We appreciate all of you taking your time to come here today. I know that our staff worked really hard to get the right group of people who can help illuminate this issue.

We are starting from our left to the right with Professor Glenn Loury, who is the Merton P. Stoltz Professor of Social Sciences at the department of economics at Brown University. He has taught previously at Boston, Harvard, and Northwestern Universities and the University of Michigan.

He is a distinguished academic economist who has contributed to a wide variety of areas in applied microeconomic theory, and has written extensively on racial inequality.

Professor Bruce Western, is the director of multidisciplinary programs in inequality and social policy at the Kennedy School of Government. He taught at Princeton from 1993 to 2007. His work has focused on the role of incarceration in social and economic inequality in American society. He is the author of "Punishment and Inequality in America: A Study of the Growth and Social Impact of the American Penal System."Alphonso Albert is the director of Second Chances in Norfolk, Virginia, a program designed to provide comprehensive support services that lead to full-time employment and social stability for those individuals impacted by the stigma of being labeled as ex-offenders.

Prior to working with Second Chances, Mr. Albert served as the assistant director of business liaison for the city of Norfolk's enterprise community initiative, Norfolk Works, Incorporated.

Dr. Michael Jacobson is the director of the Vera Institute of Justice. He is the author of "Downsizing Prisons: How to Reduce Crime and End Mass Incarceration."Prior to joining Vera, he was a professor at the City University of New York Graduate Center and the John Jay College of Criminal Justice. He served as New York City's correction commissioner, probation commissioner, and deputy budget director.

Pat Nolan is vice president of Prison Fellowship, where he focuses on efforts to ensure that offenders are better prepared to live healthy, productive, law-abiding lives on their release. He served 15 years in the California State Assembly, four of them as the Assembly Republican Leader.

Mr. Nolan has appeared before Congress to testify on matters such as prison work programs, juvenile justice, and religious freedom.

We welcome all of the witnesses. Normally, this is a 5-minute round. I think, with the depth of knowledge of the witnesses, I am prepared to go to 8 minutes, if any witness wants to go to 8 minutes.

Dr. Loury, welcome. You can begin.

STATEMENT OF DR. GLENN C. LOURY, PROFESSOR OF ECONOMICS AND SOCIAL SCIENCES, BROWN UNIVERSITY

Dr. Loury. Thank you. Mr. Chairman, Madam Vice Chairwoman, and distinguished Members, I thank you for the opportunity to address this vital issue before your Committee.

There are six main points that I wish to make with this testimony about the advent of mass incarceration as a crime control policy in the United States:

First, let me reiterate what has already been said, which is that over the past four decades, we have witnessed an historic expansion of coercive State power deployed internally on a massive scale.

As a result of this policy, the American prison system has grown into a leviathan, unmatched in human history. Never has a supposedly free country denied basic liberty to so many of its citizens.

We imprison, as has been said, at a far higher rate than any other industrial democracy in the world; we imprison at a higher rate than Russia, China, and vastly more than any of the countries in Europe.

Second, it is my considered opinion that this high level of imprisonment, is not any longer, if ever it was, a rational response to high levels of crime, rather, our mass incarceration policy is an historical inheritance bequeathed to us by wave after wave of crime fighting at the State and Federal levels over the past 35 years.

This policy response, I firmly believe, has now become counterproductive. The so-called War on Drugs, about which I will have a little bit more to say at the end of this testimony, is a leading example of one such misconceived policy initiative that now has us in its grip.

Thirdly, I wish to point out that institutional arrangements for dealing with criminal offenders in the United States, evolved to serve expressive as well as instrumental ends. This is perhaps not surprising, but it is also not an entirely healthy development.

We have wanted to send message to the criminals and to the law-abiding public alike, and we have done so with a vengeance.

In the process, we have, in effect, answered the question of who is to blame for the maladies which beset our troubled civilization? That is, we have, in effect, constructed a national narrative; we have created scapegoats; we have indulged our need to feel virtuous.

We have assuaged our fears. We have met the enemy, and the enemy is them, the violent, predatory, immoral, irredeemable thugs.

I believe that this narrative, which supports and encourages our embrace of the policy of mass incarceration, is, itself, a sociologically naive and morally superficial view about how to deal with social problems at the bottom rungs of American society.

Fourth, I feel constrained to observe that these people who have offended, as Senator Brownback said in his opening remarks, these people who have offended against our laws, are, nevertheless, human beings, and while they may deserve punishment, imprisoning them is something that we, the people of the United States of America, are doing.

Indeed, punishment is one of the most politically salient things that you can do in a democracy. The State is forcibly depriving citizens of their liberty.

Precisely how we do such a thing is a measure of our national character. And while this practice is necessary for the maintenance of order in society, it should always be undertaken humanely and in a spirit of hope, in a manner that comports with our deepest political and spiritual values.

We ought never to lose sight of the essential humanity of those whom we punish and of the humanity of those to whom offenders are connected via the intimate ties of social and psychic affiliation.

Unfortunately, we have not always lived up to this high standard.

Fifth, I must call attention to, again, as has been noted, a huge gap between the race in the incidence of punishment which exists in our country.

Black Americans and Hispanics, together, account for about one- quarter of the overall national population, but constitute about two-thirds of the State and Federal prison populations.

The extent of racial disparity in imprisonment rates, is greater than in any other area of American life. The scandalous fact of the matter is that the primary contact between poorly educated Black American men of a certain age, and the American state, is via the police and the penal apparatus.

The coercive aspect of government is the most salient feature of their experience of the public sector. My colleague sitting here, Bruce Western, has estimated, as he will say, I suppose, in greater detail, that some 59 percent of Black male high school dropouts born in the late 1960s, had been sent to prison on a felony offense at least once before they reached the age of 35.

For these men and the families and communities with which they are associated, the adverse effects of incarceration will extend well beyond their stay behind bars.

A fundamental point to bear in mind is that the experience of prison feeds back to affect the life course of those incarcerated, in an adverse manner. The vast majority of inmates do return eventually to society.

The evidence that prison has adversely affected their subsequent life chances is considerable and impressive.

Now, I invite you to consider the nearly 60 percent of Black male high school dropouts born in the late 1960s, who will have been in prison before their 40th year. For these men, their links to family have been disrupted.

Their subsequent work lives will be diminished. Their voting rights may be curtailed or even revoked. They will suffer, quite literally, civic excommunication from American democracy.

It is no exaggeration to say that, given our zeal for social discipline, these men will be consigned to a permanent, non-White male nether caste. Yet, since these men, whatever their shortcomings, have emotional and sexual and family needs, including the need to be fathers and husbands, we will have created a bio-political situation where the children of this nether caste are likely, themselves, to join a new generation of untouchables. I understand that this is harsh language, but I think it is a very harsh reality that I am describing.

In the interest of time, let me curtail reading my formal remarks here, and just say, finally, that I want to make a few observations about the War on Drugs.

This policy has not been successful, in my view, and it has a hugely disparate, adverse impact on the African American community. Consider the table, which is in your handout. It is actually taken from Professor Western's book, giving a chart showing drug offenses and arrest ratios over the period from 1970 to 2000.

What the chart shows is that in the 1970s, Blacks were arrested for drug offenses at twice the rate of Whites, and by the late 1980s, that ratio had grown to four times as great.

[The referenced chart appears in the Submissions for the Record on page 51.]

However, as another chart in your handout, the figure labeled "High School Seniors Reporting Drug Use," also drawn from Professor Western's work, shows Blacks do not use drugs at any higher rate than Whites. Black high school seniors reported using drugs at a slightly lower rate than did Whites.

[The referenced chart appears in the Submissions for the Record on page 51.]

So we have a situation where, to deal with the problem, we are punishing people, but the problem has been generated by faults and failures in our society that are very broad in terms of class and race, that do not fall with any one group.

It can be no surprise to us that if there is going to be an open-air drug market in a city, it is going to take place by the tracks, near the docks, in the dark corner, in places where people can be anonymous.

And it is going to be manned and womanned by people whose alternative opportunities are very scant, who do not have education and who do not have another way of making money. That can come as no surprise to us.

But that market would not be there in the first place if it were not for ordinary Americans, your constituents, my relatives, people like you and I, who want to engage in the consumption of these substances.

When we punish the suppliers, we weight the cost of this social malady wholly on one segment of a transaction that takes two to tango. And the racial inequality of that is really quite stark.

Let me close by giving one concrete illustration of what I am talking about. I believe there is a floor chart that gives statistics on marijuana arrests in New York City over the three decades of 1977 through 2006.

If you could display it, please, what it shows is that—this is just one city. It is an important city, of course, and we have good data for New York City, so it is possible to examine this empirically, but it is not uncharacteristic of what is going on around the country.

[The referenced chart appears in the Submissions to the Record on page 55.]

We changed our policy in the late 1980s and early 1990s, and in New York City, the crackdown on marijuana possession, was very severe. As you can see, in that decade from 1997 to 2006, 10 times as many people are being arrested for marijuana possession in the city as had been in the decade prior.

If you could show the next chart, it gives a breakdown of those arrests by race in New York City. What you will see for the city there is just what I had been saying about the national scene, which is that while the intensity of marijuana arrests increases dramatically, the burden of those arrests is borne vastly disproportionately by Black and Latino residents of the city, relative to Whites.

[The referenced chart appears in the Submissions to the Record on page 56.]

There is no reason to suppose that Blacks in New York City are consuming marijuana or any other drug at any higher a rate relative to Whites than is the national population, and we know that there is really no racial disparity, or if anything, Whites are consuming at a slightly higher rate in the national population.

This result is a consequence of policing behavior and the decisions that police are making about whom to arrest when they see them smoking marijuana in public, but I merely want to give it as a concrete illustration of the main point that I am trying to make, which is that the weight of this institutional transformation is being borne vastly disproportionately by some of the most disadvantaged people in our society, and a fundamental question of fairness is raised by that, in my mind, and I want to call it to your attention.

Finally, let me just say this about the War on Drugs: I am a economist and I cannot help take note of the fact—again, it is in your handout—that while the War on Drugs—I have a chart that says ''Winning the War: Drug Prices, Emergency Treatment, and Incarceration Rates, 1980–2000."[The referenced chart appears in the Submissions to the Record on page 52.]

I just cannot help but take note of the fact that the solid line in that chart that is moving upward over the course of those 20 years, is a measure of the number of inmates in prison for drug offenses, that has increased steadily.

The dashed line in that chart, which also moves upward over the course of those 20 years is a measure of the number of emergency room admissions of people who have gone with drug maladies to emergency rooms, and so that gives some measure of the intensity of abuse of drugs.

All the other lines in that chart are measures of the quality-adjusted price on the street, of heroin, cocaine, and methamphetamine. As you can see, with the exception of methamphetamine, which has a price spike in the late 1980s and early 1990s, all of those lines are headed straight down, which is to say that over the 20-year period from 1980 to 2000, while we have severely ratcheted up the intensity of the punishment of drug offenders, the problems from drug use have not abated—witness the emergency room admissions—and the ease of obtaining the substances on the street has not been diminished. The best measure of that is the price of the substance on the street, which has been going down, in quality-adjusted terms.

Senator Webb. Dr. Loury, we are going to have to ask you to wrap this up pretty fast.

Dr. Loury. Thank you very much for the opportunity.

[The prepared statement of Dr. Loury appears in the Submissions for the Record on page 47.]

Senator Webb. There will be further opportunities to get to those points, and we thank you very much for the eloquent testimony. Dr. Western?

STATEMENT OF DR. BRUCE WESTERN, DIRECTOR, INEQUALITY AND SOCIAL POLICY PROGRAM, KENNEDY SCHOOL OF GOVERNMENT, HARVARD UNIVERSITY

Dr. Western. Mr. Chairman and members of the Committee, thank you for the opportunity of testifying today about the causes and economic effects of the growth in the incarceration rate.

The fraction of the population in State and Federal prison has increased in every single year for the last 34 years. The rate of imprisonment today is now five times higher than in 1972. The U.S. rate of imprisonment is 5 to 10 times higher than in the longstanding democracies of Western Europe.

Internationally, our incarceration rate is only rivaled but not exceeded by the incarceration rates of South Africa and Russia.

Today's novel rates of incarceration are most remarkable for their concentration among young African American men with little schooling. To understand the prevalence of the penal system in the lives of these young men, I calculated the percentage of men who have ever been to prison by their mid-thirties.

Most prisoners will be admitted for the first time, before age 35, so this is an estimate of the lifetime chances of going to prison.

Now we are talking about prison incarceration, not jail incarceration. This is at least 12 months of time served in a State or Federal facility, for a felony conviction. It is an average of 34 months of time served.

For men born in the late 1940s, who reached their mid-thirties in 1979, Blacks were 9 percent likely to go to prison—about 1 in 10 Black men would go to prison, if they were born in the late 1940s.

For Black men born in the late 1960s, the lifetime chances of imprisonment had grown to 22.8 percent. Among Black men without a college education, now in their early forties, nearly a third have prison records, and for young Black male dropouts, prison time has become a normal life event.

A number of people have quoted this statistic today, and I estimate that about 60 percent of young Black male high school dropouts born since the late 1960s will go to prison at some point in their lives.

Young Black men are now more likely to go to prison than to graduate college with a 4-year degree, and they are more likely to go to prison today than to serve in the military.

These extraordinary rates of incarceration are new. We need only go back 20 years to find a time when the penal system was not pervasive in the lives of young African American men.

In the period of mass incarceration, Blacks have remained seven to eight times more likely to be incarcerated than Whites. This large racial disparity is unmatched by most other social indicators.

Racial disparities in unemployment, non-marital child-bearing, infant mortality, and wealth, for example, were all significantly lower than the racial disparity in imprisonment.

These high rates of incarceration have significant economic consequences. My analysis of the National Longitudinal Survey of Youth indicates that incarceration reduces hourly wages by between 10 and 15 percent, and this is in a population that has very poor economic opportunities to begin with.

Annual employment is reduced by 10 to 15 percent. Because of the combined effects on wages and annual employment, the effects on annual incomes are very large, and I find that the annual incomes of formerly incarcerated men are about 35 percent to 40 percent lower than for similar men who have not been incarcerated.

These effects of incarceration on individual economic status are not new. We can find research going back to the 1960s, providing similar results.

What is new is the scale on which these effects are now being played out. Because returning prisoners are highly concentrated in poor urban neighborhoods, the economic penalties of incarceration now permeate the most economically vulnerable families and communities.

Because incarceration rates are now so historically high, assistance for reintegration and rehabilitation will also be felt, not just by those coming out of prison, but by the poor and minority communities from which they originate.

What can we do? I suggest three types of policies would help alleviate the social and economic effects of mass incarceration: Congress should reexamine the large number of collateral consequences limiting the access of ex-felons to Federal benefits and employment.

Many restrictions, such as limitations on educational, welfare, and housing benefits, do not serve public safety, impede the reintegration of the formerly incarcerated, and penalize family members.

While restrictions on benefits or employment might be justified, if they are closely linked to particular crimes, such restrictions should be strictly time-limited, because of the strong pattern of criminal desistance with age.

Two, Congress should support prisoner re-entry programs that provide transitional employment and other services. Well-designed programs have been found to improve employment and reduce recidivism.

Research suggests that community-based re-entry programs should ideally be integrated with education and other programs in prison. Post-prison employment would be encouraged by passage of the Second Chance Act.

I am very encouraged by the remarks of the Committee on the Second Chance Act of 2007 today. Employer incentives can be promoted through expansions of the Work Opportunity Tax Credit and the Federal bonding program.

Three, Congress should support the establishment of criminal justice social impact panels in local jurisdictions, that can evaluate unwarranted disparities in juvenile and adult incarceration.

By assessing the link between socioeconomic disparities in offending and disparities in incarceration, local social impact panels could identify and take steps to eliminate disproportionate incarceration in poor and minority communities, or indeed, in any community.

My research indicates that the penal system now places a very heavy burden on poor and fragile families. But this story is largely unknown outside the communities most affected.

Robust action by Congress can change our national conversation about criminal punishment, help ensure that the great benefits of our economy are passed on to the poorest, and by doing so, will promote public safety. Thanks very much for the opportunity.

[The prepared statement of Dr. Western appears in the Submissions for the Record on page 57.]

Senator Webb. Thanks very much, Dr. Western. Alphonso Albert, who has a hands-on career, I am very interested in hearing your views, sir.

STATEMENT OF ALPHONSO ALBERT, EXECUTIVE DIRECTOR, SECOND CHANCES

Mr. Albert. Thank you. Chairman Webb, Vice Chair Maloney, Senators, Congressman Scott, thank you for having me here today.

I work in this area every day. I work with the offender every day and I see a lot of the issues and problems firsthand.

Over the past 8 years, Second Chances has served more than 1200 offenders; provided more than 900 jobs at an average wage of $9.00 an hour; maintained more than a 73-percent retention rate for employment over 2 years, and something I neglected to include in my written statement, but after listening to Senator Brownback, I was reminded to include that we have maintained less than a 10-percent recidivism rate over the 8-year period, and that is for the entire 1200 that we have served.

We have initiated or implemented programs that work with children of incarcerated parents in providing tutoring, cultural outings, exposing them to alternative kinds of things.

We have instituted a housing initiative for offenders that are returning, that are homeless. It is a permanent supportive housing initiative.

We jointly collaborated with one of our late local State funders and the city of Norfolk, and implemented a housing program.

We have implemented three business enterprises where we hire offenders at a minimum wage of $8 an hour, and if they are able to get their license—and we help them get that, because that is a major challenge. A drivers license and ID when they leave prison is a major challenge and a major obstacle.

When they get a drivers license, we are able to pay them $12 an hour with benefits. It is a moving company, a landscaping company, and a building maintenance company that we have initiated to employ the offenders ourselves, aside from working with local employers.

There is a collateral cost, I think, to incarceration that largely goes unspoken. And let me just say, before I get fully into my presentation, that I wholeheartedly agree with the recommendations of Dr. Western.

He really touched on some significant points that I think we do not often think about when we talk about providing services to offenders, supporting re-entry initiatives, and the kinds of recommendations that he made earlier.

But the cost is one to the families, and most offenders that we see, actually, I believe, all come from a family, but most have families. One of the reasons that the stats that Senator Brownback quoted about a family member is five times more likely to be incarcerated themselves, is because the same conditions that existed for that offender will exist for that family member unless there is some intervening factor that we try to disrupt, if you will.

It is not because those people are predisposed to incarceration, but they are going to come up in the same conditions. The children are going to come up in the same conditions, they are going to be under-educated, have limited employment opportunities, with the same influences around them, and so they are subject to the same outcome and same results.

The greatest challenge that we face on a daily basis in working with the offenders is lack of pre-release planning and post-release services; pre-release planning, because the expectation of the offender is often quite different when they seek to get out, and the expectations of probation and parole, if they have a probation officer, if they happen to have any parole, which is getting less and less likely, the expectation of how helpful that parole officer will be, what family members will be.

We have instituted housing laws that are discriminatory, which makes it difficult for an offender to even go back and connect with his family.

I know, locally, in the city of Norfolk, with our local housing authority, if an offender were to try to use his family as a stabilizing source or force, whereas most people that get in life crisis or life challenge or difficulty can go to family, he cannot. He cannot be seen connected with the family.

He cannot go into that community again. Private-sector housing persons are able to discriminate, based on him having a record, so it is less and less likely that he can even get an apartment or place of his own, even if he has resources.

Recently, the State of Virginia became one of seven States around the country to participate in the National Governors Association Re-entry Policy Academy. Virginia subsequently initiated five pilot programs around the State, but they have done so with no funding.

And with no funding, there are no counselors to initiate pre-release planning, there is no funding to support post-releases services to help people with case management, to help people with job placement, job referrals, life skills training, any kind of skills training that creates a situation where the person is better off coming out than they were going in.

Those are some of the challenges that we face. I would venture to say, at the legislative level, both locally, statewide, and federally, we have had an approach that sort of advocates revenge as opposed to exacting public justice.

It seems that we advocate for revenge, and so we get systems— and when we work with offenders, like local circuit court systems, collection agencies that seem content on exacting greater levels of punishment, they feel compelled to perpetuate the punishment, like, I want to be a part of this that makes it more difficult for you to make a transition, so that the offender gets no support.

If he is trying to get a collection on how many court costs and fines he has, child support enforcement, that locks him up when he is not working and says it is voluntary unemployment, so he cannot earn money to pay off child support that he is already amassed.

And so it seems that at every level, somebody else is exacting more punishment. I will say this one last thing, Senator Webb: A young lady came into my office. She was a part of our program for a long time, and she has become a part of a group we call the Advocates for Second Chances, and she advocates for other people that are going through life transition in the peer support group.

And she had been recently turned down for a license to get her nursing license. She had gone to school, she had gone through all the hoops, she had lost two jobs the year before, and she came in my office and she sat down and she started crying.

She asked me, she said, it has been 18 years and I would like to know, when is the debt paid? At what point is this debt going to be paid?

And I think a lot of our offenders face that daily, where there seems to be no end to the punishment. Thank you.

[The prepared statement of Mr. Albert appears in the Submissions for the Record on page 65.]

Senator Webb. Thank you very much, Mr. Albert. I couldn't agree more with what you just said.

Dr. Jacobson, welcome.

STATEMENT OF DR. MICHAEL P. JACOBSON, DIRECTOR, VERA INSTITUTE OF JUSTICE

Dr. Jacobson. Thank you, and good morning Senator Webb, Vice Chair Maloney, and to the rest of the Committee members for inviting me here today.

The United States now spends over $60 billion annually to maintain its Corrections System, reflecting the fact that we imprison— as we have heard many times today—a greater percentage of our population than any other nation on earth.

In the last 30 years we have seen our jail and prison population rise from almost 250,000 to almost 2.3 million currently, nearly a tenfold increase. The strain that this geometric increase in those incarcerated puts on our States and cities is cumulative and continues to grow.

Over the last decade and a half, the only function of State governments that has grown as a percentage of overall State budgets is, with the exception of Medicaid, corrections. The rate of growth of spending on corrections in State budgets exceeds that for education, health care, social services, transportation, and environmental protection.

There is a very clear relationship between the amount of money we spend on prisons and the amount that is available, or not available, for all these other essential areas of government. In many States—and California is one that specifically comes to mind—one can literally see money move in the budget from primary and secondary education to prisons.

State budgets tend to be largely zero-sum games, and increases in corrections spending have absolutely held down spending in these other areas of government, many of which are also directly related to public safety.

Of course the obvious question this raises is: What do we get for that money? Certainly there should be some significant connection between our tremendous use of prison and public safety.

As most people know, the United States experienced a large crime decline from the early 1990s to the early 2000s, and it would seem to make intuitive sense that our significantly increasing prison systems played a major role in that decline.

In fact, it is a far more mixed story than it appears. There is consensus among criminologists and social scientists that over the last decade our increased use of prison was responsible for only some— maybe one-fifth, but by no means most— of the national crime decline.

Additionally, there is also agreement that going forward putting even more people in prison will have declining effectiveness as we put more and more people in prison who present less and less of a threat to public safety.

At this point, putting greater numbers of people into prison as a way to achieve more public safety is one of the least effective ways we know of to decrease crime.

We know, for instance, that even after spending tens of billions of dollars on incarceration, more than half of those leaving prison are back in prison within 3 years, not a result that anyone should be proud of.

We know that targeted spending for effective in-prison and post- prison re-entry programs will reduce crime, and thus the number of victims, more substantially than any prison expansion. We know that diverting people who are not threats to public safety from prison into serious and structured community-based alternatives to prison is more effective than simply continuing to incarcerate these same people at huge expense.

In the same vein, research shows that increasing high school graduation rates, certain neighborhood-based law enforcement initiatives, and increases in employment and wages will also more effectively reduce crime than a greater use of prison.

We also know that incarcerating so much of our population, and especially the disproportionate incarceration of people of color, comes with other costs as well. We have heard many of them already.

Hundreds of thousands of people leave prison annually with no right to vote, no access to public housing, hugely limited ability to find employment, and high levels of drug use and mental illness.

These unintended consequences of incarceration ripple through families and communities as those returning home are overwhelmed by seemingly intractable obstacles. Not surprisingly, astounding numbers wind up returning to prison, further draining scarce resources that could be made available to deal with some of these obstacles themselves.

As someone who used to run the largest city jail system in the country, I know that most people who leave jail and prison do not want to go back. It is a miserable and degrading experience, and my colleagues who run these systems and I always marvel about the number of people who, once they leave prison, want to make good and do good.

Once they leave, however, they are confronted by such overwhelming barriers on which we currently spend almost no money or attention that no one should be surprised when these same people return to prison so soon.

We know that States can continue to decrease crime and simultaneously decrease prison populations. New York State, for example, for the last 7 years has seen the largest decrease in its prison population of any State in the country—a decline of 14 percent.

The rest of the States increased their prison populations by an average of 12 percent over the same time period, and many States increased far more than that.

At that same time, violent crime decreased in New York State by 20 percent compared to just over 1 percent for the rest of the country.

Prison populations can drop, along with crime and victimization. If we were serious about using our limited resources most effectively to reduce crime and victimization and increase public safety, then we would begin to responsibly and systematically transfer to community-based prevention, re-entry, and capacity building some of the resources now used to imprison people.

It is important to stress here that this is an issue of public safety. Even putting aside all arguments about efficiency and effectiveness, talking only in terms of public safety, we will all be safer if we begin to re-invest into other programmatic initiatives both inside and outside the criminal justice system some of the money that now goes to incarcerate people who do not pose a threat to public safety and who, in fact, become more of a threat to public safety once they have been imprisoned.

The fact is that almost all the extant research points out that our prison system is too big, too expensive, drains funds away from other essential areas that can more effectively increase public safety, and is harmful to our poorest communities.

Despite all this research, however, we continue to imprison more and more people. There are a host of reasons for this ongoing trend, including the attraction of prisons as engines of economic development for rural communities, the financial incentives for public employee unions as well as for the private prison industry in spending more on prisons, the realities of the budget process and constrained budgets that limit opportunities to make substantial investments in new initiatives, and the omnipresent hyper-politics that surround issues of crime and punishment in the United States.

These are all formidable obstacles, but none should be sufficient to keep us from educating policymakers and the public that there is a better way to be safe and have less crime. Thank you.

[The prepared statement of Dr. Jacobson appears in the Submissions for the Record on page 66.]

Senator Webb. Thank you very much.

Mr. Nolan, welcome.

Statement of Pat Nolan, Vice President, Prison Fellowship

Mr. Nolan. Thank you.

Mr. Chairman and Members, I appreciate very much this opportunity to share my thoughts with you on the costs of the massive increase in incarceration in the United States. As Mr. Chairman mentioned, I am vice president of Prison Fellowship and served in the California Legislature for 15 years, 4 of those as Republican leader. I was reliably tough on crime legislator.

I was one of the original sponsors of the Victims Bill of Rights and was awarded the Victims Advocate Award by Parents of Murdered Children.

Then I was prosecuted for a campaign contribution I accepted which turned out to be part of an F.B.I. sting, and I served 29 months in Federal custody.

Now God has placed me in a position of Prison Fellowship that allows me to share my observation with government officials like you to use my experience as a lawyer, a legislator, and a prisoner to improve our system.

The figures on incarceration are staggering. One in every 32 adult Americans is in prison or on supervised release—1 in every 32.

Prisons have become the fastest growing item in State budgets, siphoning off dollars that could otherwise be available for schools, roads, and hospitals. Offenders serve their sentences in overcrowded prisons where they are exposed to the horrors of violence, including rape; isolation from family and friends; and despair.

The best way I can describe to you how it feels to be in prison is: I was an amputee. I was cut off from my family, from my home, from my community, from my job, and from my church. Then, with my stumps still bleeding, I was tossed into a roiling cauldron of anger, bitterness, despair, and often violence.

Most inmates are idle in prison, warehoused with little preparation to make better choices when they return to the free world. Just one-third of all released prisoners will receive vocational or educational training in prison.

While about 3 of every 4 prisoners has a substance abuse problem, less than 20 percent will receive any drug-abuse treatment while they are incarcerated.

The number of returning inmates is now four times what it was just 20 years ago, yet there are fewer programs to prepare them for a successful return to our communities.

On leaving prisons they will have difficulty finding employment. The odds are great that they will return to prison. More than 700,000 inmates will be released next year from our prisons. To put that in context: That is three times the size of the United States Marine Corps. Over 1900 felons a day will be released from prisons and returned home.

What has been done to prepare them to live healthy, productive lives? What kind of neighbors will they be? Our large investment in prisons might be justified if inmates were reformed in their hearts and their habits, but most inmates do not leave prisons transformed into law-abiding citizens.

In fact, the very skills they learn inside to survive make them anti-social when they come home. The fact of the matter is that if things continue as they are, most of the inmates released will commit more crimes.

Over the last 30 years, the rate of recidivism has remained steadily at about two-thirds. If two-thirds of the patients leaving a hospital went home sick, we would find a better way to treat them.

We have to find a better way to help inmates change their lives so they can live safely in the community.

One important step would be to pass the Second Chance Act. I am delighted that so many members on the dais are co-sponsors of it. We are very close to passing it. It will help our States and communities develop ways to prepare inmates for their safe and successful transition home.

But in addition to prison preparation, we must also examine the sentencing statutes that put so many nonviolent offenders in prison. Certainly we need prisons to separate the dangerous offenders from our society. But given the overcrowding and violence in our prisons, why on earth would we send a nonviolent person to prison?

Prisons are for people we are afraid of. Yet our sentencing laws have filled them with people we are just mad at.

Changing our sentences so that low-risk offenders are punished in the community under strict supervision would reduce overcrowding in prisons and help control the violence. It would hold low-risk offenders accountable without exposing them to violence and the great difficulties of transitioning back to employment in the community after their sentence.

The moment after offenders step off the bus, they face several critical decisions:

> Where will they live?
> Where can they get a meal?
> Where should they look for a job?
> How do they get to the job interview?
> And where can they earn enough money just to pay for the necessities of life?

Returning inmates are also confronted with many details that are just personal business, for example, obtaining ID cards. Why on earth would we send inmates home from prison without an ID or a license? We know who they are.

Some States—Alabama, for instance, gives them a check for $5, but no ID. Now how do you cash that check when you get home?

Making medical appointments is extremely difficult for them, as is working through the many bureaucratic problems of everyday life. Individually they are difficult. Taken together, they can be overwhelming.

The difficulties that inmates face prompt intense stress, and they worry about the logistics of just getting by. To someone who has had no control over their lives for a period of years, it floods them with too much, too many decisions to make.

My own experience is a good example. The day I came to the halfway house, a bunch of my buddies from the capitol took me to the 8th Street Deli. They all ordered. The waiter stood there. I knew what I was supposed to do, but my eyes raced over the menu and I was paralyzed. I couldn't decide what to order.

For 2 years I had not had a choice over what to eat. So finally, out of embarrassment, I just ordered what my eyes lit upon just to get that humiliation over with.

Now, think about the person that leaves prison that did not come from a good family, that did not have my education, that did not have the strong faith I had. How do they deal with all these issues? Issues of life and death in many cases. That's what confronts them. And we do so little to prepare them.

I realize I am running out of time. I would just like to make a couple of extra points. One is the importance of mentors and the Second Chance Act as a grant program to help community and faith-based groups establish mentoring programs.

What at-risk people need are loving people to help them with all these decisions I just discussed. Dr. King said: "To change someone, you must first love them and they must know that they are loved."The government and its programs cannot love a person; only people can do that. So we really need to encourage volunteers, most of which come from churches, synagogues, and mosques, to come along beside these people and invest in them.

Prison Fellowship for 31 years has served prisoners, ex-prisoners, and their families. We have found six things that are essential.

One is: Community. Put men and women in facilities, in dorms, housing units, where those that want to change their lives can have a community free from the usual prison atmosphere.

Second: Consistency. Being able to work with them on a consistent and frequent basis—daily if possible.

Third: Character. A focus on moral and personal issues that led to criminal behavior. The inmates need a moral compass to help them make the decision when they get out. They say "character"is doing what is right when no one is looking. We have to help them understand why that is important.

Fourth: It is comprehensive. It should focus on transformation of every aspect of their lives: Spiritual formation, education, vocational training, substance abuse treatment, life skill training, and parental skills.

Fifth: It should be continuous. It should start in prison - *Senator Webb*. Mr. Nolan, we are going to have to ask you to summarize your remarks.

Mr. Nolan. As a State legislator I made the mistake of thinking that locking up more people would automatically make us safer. Only when I was in prison did I realize that imprisoning so many of our people while doing little to prepare them to come home actually makes us less safe.

When two out of three inmates are arrested within 3 years of release, our criminal justice system is failing us. Prisons do not exist as an end in themselves. They exist to make our communities safer. We must hold them accountable to do that.

I am grateful to God that I live in the United States so that Inmate 06833097 can come and testify before Congress and express my opinions without fear of arrest. And I am so grateful to all of you for caring enough to hold this hearing and try to start a public discussion of this serious problem that confronts us.

Thank you.

[The prepared statement of Mr. Nolan appears in the Submissions for the Record on page 68.]

Senator Webb. Thank you very much, Mr. Nolan, for your testimony. I appreciate all of the testimony today. It has been very eloquent, and I appreciate the patience of our colleagues here. We all have to run according to the clock, but there is so much valuable information that we need to be listening to, so I did extend the clock quite a bit.

I will begin our question period. We will go down the line and have more than one round, if people want to ask further questions.

I would like to just quickly start off by saying I became interested in this on a policy level about 25 years ago when I was, to my knowledge, the first American journalist who was able to get inside the Japanese jail system. I did a story for Parade Magazine about Americans in Japanese Jails.

At that time, even though I had been a committee counsel here, and I had a law degree, it was the first time that I really sat down and read—I read all of the Bureau of Justice Statistics about crime in the United States to try to make a comparison, and there were a couple of things that jumped out at me at that point.

One was that Japan had a population half the United States, one-half exactly at that time, and they only had 40,000 people in jail. They had 50,000 people under government control, 10,000 awaiting resolution of their cases. But at that time we had 780,000 people in jail, and we were probably second in the world in terms of the incarceration rate. Now we have got more than 2 million people in jail.

I have followed this over the years, and I am grateful that I have had the opportunity to be able to start to work on this process, and I am committed to trying to do something about this not just today in this hearing but in the future.

One of the things that needs to happen in my opinion, whenever you start trying to turn policies around, is that the American public needs to understand the dimensions of the problem, the cultural dimensions of the problem rather than simply going to one bill or another bill.

In the testimony today there were a couple of things that had come up. And Dr. Loury you were very specific about this in your writings, which I have found to be incredibly perceptive.

Karl Zinsmeister, who works in the White House now.

Vice Chair Maloney. Chairman Webb, we have a series of votes in the House, so we—

Senator Webb. Would you like to say something before you go, then?

Vice Chair Maloney. I just would like to—

Senator Webb. I will interrupt my questions and—

Vice Chair Maloney. Just 2 seconds to welcome very strongly Dr. Jacobson, who has served with great distinction in the city in which I live, and I know him from my city council days. Congratulations on your service. I thought all of your testimony was very moving, and we want to do something about it. But right now we have got to go vote and we will try to get back, but thank you.

Senator Webb. Well thank you very much for coming over, and I hope we can work on this more in the future.

Two pieces come together, and I would like to get your reactions on this: One is that Karl Zinsmeister was saying at a panel—he works for President Bush now, he used to be the editor of American Enterprise Magazine and had worked for Senator Moynihan at one point—he was talking about the fact that family stability is a key indicator to success in America.

And what we see here when you are discussing the adverse effects of the avalanche that continues down when we go into incarceration is the incredible impact on and the destruction of the family, particularly in the Black community right now.

A second piece that I find very persuasive—and I would like to get your reactions to—is this notion, and Dr. Loury you mentioned it specifically with your charts up here—that particularly in drug cases, the point of arrest seems to identify who the criminal is, rather than the conduct itself. You go into these neighborhoods where drugs are being sold, and the abnormality of, or the skewing of, the statistics becomes a function of where the arrests are made. The arrests are made in a specific spot because that is where the drugs are sold, which tends to skew the prison population—I would like to get your further thoughts on both of those points.

We could just start down the panel, any way you want to discuss them. I think the American public needs to understand both of those.

Dr. Loury. Well, let me just take this opportunity, in response to the question to call attention to some charts that I wanted to show during my testimony but did not have an opportunity to, which is a geographical map of New York City, "Changes In Spatial Concentration of Incarceration In New York City."[The referenced chart appears in the Submissions for the Record on page 53.]

So there is the chart. This is drawn from the work of the sociologists at Columbia University, the criminologist Jeffrey Fagan and his colleagues.

Basically what is shown there are the areas (in red) with the highest concentration of persons incarcerated in New York State, who lived in New York City prior to their incarceration.

The Black area is the next-highest level of concentration. And you can see there is a very geographically specific pattern to where people live in the city who end up going to prison from the city: certain neighborhoods in the north of Manhattan, in the south of Bronx, in Brooklyn, and in Queens. That was 1985 on the left panel. The right panel is 1996.

What you see is that the areas of high concentration in 1985 are also areas of high concentration in 1996, but they have grown bigger; this shows that the epidemiology—the spatial pattern—of incarceration has a very clear structure in these particular areas of the city.

The authors of the study from which that figure is drawn go on to observe that one consequence of this is that people who live in those neighborhoods who are incarcerated, once they are released from prison, come back to those neighborhoods; that police officers in pursuit of criminals are disproportionately—

Senator Webb. Excuse me, Dr. Loury, may I interrupt you one second?

Dr. Loury. Yes. Am I taking too much time?

Senator Webb. Congressman Hinchey has to leave for votes, and I wanted to give him an opportunity to make any statements—

Dr. Loury. Yes, of course.

Senator Webb [continuing]. Or ask any questions before he leaves.

Representative Hinchey. Well, Senator Webb, I thank you very much once again. And, Dr. Loury, please excuse the interruption.

Dr. Loury. Not at all.

Representative Hinchey. Sorry we're having this series of votes, but they are going to take another 40 minutes before they are over. We have six votes coming up, unfortunately.

I just want to express my appreciation to you for bringing our attention to this issue, and for all of you and the testimonies that you have given.

The focus of that testimony has largely been on the impacts that these circumstances and this structure has on the individuals, their families, and to a large extent also on our society.

I would like to focus attention on one other aspect of this. That is, the causes. The causes of these high rates of incarceration, and the solutions that we should be addressing ourselves to try to reduce these high rates of incarcerations.

I think one of the problems that we confront is the definition of crime, which was altered dramatically, as you pointed out, all of you, in the mid-1970s and from there on, the so-called War on Drugs, for example, is a creation that was put into place largely for political purposes, I believe, and I think that that really needs to be addressed.

So many of the people—the largest percentage, I believe, of the people that we have in prison across the country both State and Federal are based upon offenses dealing with the drug issue. And the "War on Drugs" reminds me of the establishment of Prohibition back in the 1920s, and that created a huge influx of various sorts of crime and disruption within our entire society.

So I think that these are some of the things that we need to address, and I would like very much to be able to work with you, Senator, or both of you—I know you are both strongly committed to this issue—and I hope that we can come up with some solutions. So once again, thank you.

Senator Webb. We appreciate your support. Hopefully we can get the House interested in the Second Chances Act as a starting point on this.

Representative Hinchey. Yes, indeed.

Senator Webb. Thank you very much, Congressman.

I did not mean to interrupt you.

Dr. Loury. Not at all, and I think I may have been going on. I want to give others the chance. May I just comment briefly on your reference to Mr. Zinsmeister and the issue of the family.

What I want to say about that is: Yes, of course strong families are a very good thing, and where families are strong criminal offending can be expected to be less. But the other thing that I want to add is that association is not causation.

One point that I think we need to be clear about here is that sometimes common factors can be both undermining the strength of the family and promoting criminal participation in the population.

So, you know, it would be wonderful if the family were stronger, particularly within the African American community, but it may be a mistake to say: Oh, if we could only strengthen the family, then everything would be all right. Because, as I have said, the fact that common factors of disadvantage, and stress, and economic marginality may be both undermining family relations and promoting criminality.

Senator Webb. Thank you very much.

Dr. Western, do you have any thoughts on this?

Dr. Western. Three quick thoughts on the family, Senator:

The men in prison are much more likely to have low levels of education, poor work histories, and to be economically disadvantaged in a whole variety of ways, but they are not any less likely to have children than the rest of the population. So they are as connected to children in that sense as the rest of the population.

The implication of this is that these very high rates of incarceration are creating very high rates of paternal incarceration. So there are very large numbers of children now who are experiencing a parent being sent to prison, and they parallel the figures that we have seen for incarceration rates for adults.

Incarceration is very stigmatic. The stigma of incarceration, the loss in social status, ethnographic evidence shows is passed on to children.

As well, incarceration is associated—the third point with increased risk of divorce and separation. So this run-up in the incarceration rate has been tremendously corrosive of family structure in the poor communities most affected.

On drug arrests, very quickly, drug regulation is a very different category of crime from all others. We do not have good figures on the level of drug use in the population. There are surveys, but the main figures we rely on are arrest rates.

And arrest rates are produced largely through policy decisions about policing and not underlying patterns of offending.

Where drugs are traded in public space, as they are in urban areas, rather than in private spaces, they are in suburban homes, we are going to see patterns of policing, I think, that are going to generate these very large racial disparities that we saw in the statistics that Professor Loury presented.

So I think these trends in drug arrests we see do not reflect trends in underlying behavior, but they are very much produced by decisions about policing. And because of the nature of the drug trade, that significantly explains the racial disparities we have observed.

Senator Webb. I think it is important for the American public to understand that. That is one reason I wanted to flag it. As you reach for a solution, this is not a pattern of behavior so much as it is a pattern of arrest, quite frankly.

Dr. Western. I think that is absolutely correct.

Senator Webb. Mr. Albert, would you like to add anything on this?

Mr. Albert. Just the fact, Senator Webb, that I think a lot does happen at arrest. I happen to sit on a local committee that is grant-funded to look at something called "Disproportionate Minority Contact." And one of the challenges, I think, to this Committee is assigning blame without assigning blame: Looking at every point in the process where there is a decision to be made about how to charge someone. What type of offense to charge a person with, if there is indeed an offense that has been committed? And this is affecting juveniles, but I think the same holds true for adults.

At the decision-making point, at every point in the system, the decision consistently is made in the extreme for minorities, and I think that gets the results that we see today.

Now at some point something drives that. And I think a lot of it has to do with perception. I think a lot of it has to do with living patterns. I think a lot of it has to do with our decisions about where to allocate resources; the quality-of-life kinds of calls for service, and all of a sudden that becomes a problem neighborhood.

It is easier to see certain things that cost more resources to investigate when people are able to do things inside their home, in closed communities, and so it is an easy issue to address.

So it is one of those things for me that is both simple and complicated at the same time. I think it is simple to see and understand, but very complicated to address.

Senator Webb. Dr. Jacobson? Mr. Nolan?

Dr. Jacobson. Yes, two quick points. One is on the relatively low-level drug arrests issue, in addition to all the issues that have been raised here.

Compared to having almost no one in State prisons for drug offenses 20 years ago, there are probably something like 300,000 people there now. Again, if you look at the extant research, drug sale and possession cases are crimes for which criminologists tend to feel that incarceration provides absolutely no public safety benefit.

It is very different from incarcerating someone who commits violent crimes or someone who is a rapist. There you are obviously deterring that behavior. The person is in prison. There is hopefully some general deterrence.

When you imprison what is usually some young kid dealing drugs on the street corner, you get what criminologists tend to call a one-for-one replacement. With that person in prison, there is an economic opportunity. It is a job. Someone else takes up that activity.

So you wind up spending incredible sums of money making people worse when they come out and getting essentially nothing from it except harm.

The other point that I would like to make related to all of this is: If you look at Professor Loury's charts up there, which happen to represent New York City but that could represent any city in this country, they all have the same patterns. There are incredibly concentrated geographic areas of mostly cities' poorest residents, and primarily communities of color that have huge numbers of people go up and back to State prison.

If you look at where those residents come from, how many there are, and the percentage they make up of the State prison population, New York State spends— and this is true in every State— hundreds of millions of dollars on the residents of those poorest communities. We just do not spend any of that money in those communities. We take people out of those communities, and we spend that money to hold them upstate.

And as long as we continue spending money on prisons instead of spending it on strengthening those communities and building them up, this cycle will continue.

This gets back to my point about using the money we now spend differently. We spend huge amounts of money on people who live in the poorest areas in any city. It's just that the money does not go to those areas, it goes to different areas.

Senator Webb. Thank you. I apologize for going over, Senator Casey, but we had those interruptions.

Senator Casey. That is OK.

Senator Webb [continuing]. One more thought, and then I'll turn it over to you.

Mr. Nolan. I will be quick. Two things.

One thing is: It should be the focus of our prison system to maintain and strengthen family ties. Sadly, it is the opposite. We place prisoners far from their families; oftentimes make it impossible, especially for the poor families, to visit.

We treat families very disrespectfully when they come to visit. The visitation facilities are terrible. Hours are short. We have astronomical phone costs which make it hard to stay in touch that way.

While I was in prison, I tried to read to my children over the phone. I would go over their report cards. I would read books they were reading in school. Now the Federal system limits the number of calls, and limits the number of phone numbers on inmates' call lists.

Prison Fellowship has a program called Angel Tree that reaches out to children with a gift from their incarcerated parent. It is important that we keep those family bonds strong. We should do more to knit those bonds together.

Another program in New York City La Bodega de la Familia, which aims at healing the whole family. They deal with the incarcerated parent, the spouse, girlfriend, or whatever, and children on the outside to reconcile them—there are oftentimes anger issues and frustration with the crime. They deal with codependency and actual dependency to try to ensure there is a welcoming home for them to come to.

The last thing is Mr. Hinchey brought up the definition of "crime." When our Nation was founded there were four crimes: piracy—Federal crimes—piracy, counterfeiting, treason, I'm missing one. Anyway, there are now over 4,000 statutory crimes, and tens of thousands of regulations that are de facto crimes that there doesn't have to be criminal intent, you are just convicted of them.

There is a group left and right called "Over-Criminalized.org,"which includes the National Association of Criminal Defense Council, Heritage Foundation, ACLU, and Prison Fellowship. The group is looking at why do we have all these laws that make criminals of what are essentially normal relations between people? And why do we have so many laws that put people in prison for things that are just decisions of society that "we don't like this," as opposed to being inherently evil or bad.

Senator Webb. Thank you.

I would like to note at this point that a statement from Congresswoman Sheila Jackson-Lee will be entered into the hearing record. I neglected to say that earlier.

[The prepared statement of Representative Sheila Jackson-Lee appears in the Submissions for the Record on page 73.]

Senator Webb. Senator Casey, thank you for your patience, sir. Senator Casey. Thank you, Senator Webb. I appreciate you calling this hearing.

I guess we will continue the left to right movement here.

Dr. Loury, I wanted to ask you about something you testified to. I took a quick note, and I am not sure I got it all, but part of your testimony talked about the increase in the number of arrests—and I know you spoke to that a couple of times—but also the dramatic rise in emergency room admissions.

Can you go back to that and just reiterate what you said about that, because it is a pretty dramatic fact.

Dr. Loury. Yes, I can. I had the chart called "Winning The War? Drug Prices, Emergency Treatment, and Incarceration Rates." It is not a floor chart; it was just on the handout.

[The referenced chart appears in the Submissions to the Record on page 52.]

Senator Casey. Oh, that is what it was. I think when you referred to it I did not have the handouts. I do not know if there is a—

Dr. Loury. Yes, sir. There is a handout, and there is a chart here that is taken from the research of John Caulkins and his colleagues at Carnegie Mellon University, and it basically tries to measure over the 20-year period of 1980 to 2000 both the extent of incarceration and emergency room admissions for drug-related maladies.

That is the dashed line in the chart there. The solid line is imprisonment, numbers of persons in prison for drug offenses. And then it juxtaposes with those trends the trend in the same time period of the quality-adjusted price of drugs on the streets of American cities, as best one could estimate it, and my point was simply to say that the solid line for imprisonment goes up. The dashed line for emergency room admissions goes up. But the lines for the prices are going down.

What that is telling me is that we are incarcerating more people, but as has just been noted here, you lock up someone who is selling drugs, but you don't get rid of the market, you just create an opportunity for someone else to sell drugs.

So we have not been effective at raising the price of drugs on the street; nor have we been effective at keeping people from getting and abusing the drugs in the sense that at least one indicator of that—emergency room admissions shows itself to be trending upward over this period.

So that is what I was trying to say.

Senator Casey. No, I appreciate that. And this is a great chart to have—of course it is always better if there is color, but we can work on a chart—but it really is a dramatic presentation, that even though arrests are up, ER admissions are up as well, and the price question is significant as well.

I guess I want to play devil's advocate. I guess for the whole panel. Look, if someone is watching this hearing and they see the charts we have had, and they see the testimony just on the possession issue, or arrests for possession, they may be watching. And I am not sure I fully understand some of the points that we are trying to make here.

They may be watching or listening, and they say: Well, look, if a law enforcement official encounters someone on the street and there is a law in place that you are supposed to arrest someone who has a controlled substance on them, and they arrest them, and that number keeps getting bigger, what are we arguing about here? Why is that a problem?

And I think most people can differentiate and place a greater weight on, or understand the reason we penalize those who sell drugs maybe at a higher intensity than we penalize those who are, quote, "only" in possession, but (a) how do you deal with the devil's advocate question about: Look, they were possessing a substance, and they are arrested for it, and the numbers are going up. That is one question.

But then how also do you deal with the other question, which is: Where is the problem there? Is the problem with the policy of arrest? Or is the problem with what happens after they are arrested? Or that we are locking too many of them up for, quote, "only" possession as opposed to selling?

I guess there are two big questions there. One is the devil's advocate question. And the other is where is the problem with the policy.

I don't know if I'm throwing it out to all of you, but each of you I know has some experience with these questions. Anybody.

Mr. Albert. I can speak—

Senator Casey. Mr. Albert.

Mr. Albert. Thank you. I can speak very briefly to something we see with some low-level kinds of things. I will use as an example a marijuana arrest.

The police officer has the discretion to, say, take a person to jail, in which case they have to post bail. And they risk some other kinds of factors like staying in jail a long time. If he's employed, risk losing employment. Being separated from his family if he can't post bail. Or, to give him a summons to appear in court, and then have the judge, once he appears in court with the summons, give him some kind of community alternative as opposed to incarceration.

If the decision is made to arrest him and he cannot post bail, then his life is more complicated. He is in jail obviously longer. It costs the system more, obviously, to incarcerate him. He risks losing a job if he has one, and disrupting his family.

The judge is more likely to sentence him to incarceration if he comes in front of the judge—and I am not an academician; I have not studied this, but I can tell you from my personal experiences from what I see in dealing with the people, if a person comes before the judge already incarcerated, he is more likely to be incarcerated by the judge if he is found guilty.

If he comes in from the street as a result of a summons, or having posted bail, then there is a greater likelihood—and this is purely anecdotal—that he will be given an alternative, and not be incarcerated.

So that is one example of how the decision at the point of contact is made that really starts the ball rolling. Once in jail, then there is a whole other set of factors that kicks in I think that sort of continues to exacerbate the issue.

Senator Casey. Well that example helps me a lot to understand this better. How do we change that? Not that we can enact laws to impact every decision a police officer makes, but is that because there is a uniformity in how to treat that particular offender at the street level? Or is it really that we have to focus on what police officers are told about their discretion when it comes to a first-time possession situation? Or what do you think it is?

Mr. Albert. I think police—and again I am purely speaking from my understanding of it—I think the police tend to—

Senator Casey. Well you have had a lot of experience. You have dealt with a lot of these programs, and this is valuable.

Mr. Albert. Sure. I think police tend to, in their decision making, reflect the sentiment of their community. And I think if a police officer sees a community going toward, or in the direction of an alternative to sentencing and an understanding of these kinds of things, if they see funding directed toward a program that sort of supports alternatives to incarceration and not sort of being quite as aggressive at the point of incarceration, they tend to make decisions that affect that.

I am just starting an office for the city of Norfolk called the Office of Public and Criminal Justice for the city. The idea that the city manager wanted to move forward with the entire city is that communities need justice. The kids deserve the same right to an opportunity for education and not live under the threat of gunfire. But in the context of that, we see police officers who are adjusting the way they police, interacting with the community a different way because they tend to reflect, I think, the sentiment of their community.

If they feel the community wants them to get extremely aggressive and tough at the point of contact, then I think they tend to do that. So I think as we support alternative programs, alternative to incarceration, as we support sort of these tactics that are not as aggressive with nonviolent offenses that tend to help people be more productive on the outside as opposed to incarceration, I think their mindsets tend to reflect that in their policing tactics and discretion.

Senator Casey. Thank you.

Dr. Jacobson. I think one other—

Senator Casey. Mr. Jacobson.

Dr. Jacobson [continuing]. Piece of that response to a person who asks, "What's wrong with it" , even absent the initial look at what police are making arrests for and how they use their discretion, addressing the assumption that once arrests have been made that it is perfectly appropriate to use jails and prisons for a variety of behaviors and crimes.

It is just not appropriate to use prison or jail for almost every behavior in crime. But we tend to use prison and jail as our default punishment. That is what we do. It happens to be an exceedingly expensive, punitive, and potentially harmful punishment. So you have to be really careful how you use it.

So part of the answer to, "What is wrong with putting people in jail or prison once you arrest them", is that the safety of the very person asking that question is affected if we put too many people in jail and prison. Because we are not dealing with their sobriety issues or their drug issues or their employment issues. And we know if we put people in jail or prison for relatively short periods of time, they are just going to be worse when they come out.

The person raising these issues is going to be more at risk of being victimized, but we cannot afford to spend money on the programs we know would work better because we are putting everyone in jail and prison.

So, it is a difficult decision to make. Governments should be very careful and parsimonious about how they make it. We tend to make the decision too easily for everyone because it works at some political level. It just does not work at a substantive level.

Senator Casey. Mr. Nolan?

Mr. Nolan. As a conservative I was suspicious of every branch of government—OSHA, DMV, CalTrans—

[Laughter.]

Mr. Nolan. But I turned a blind eye to law enforcement and prosecutors. I guess, thinking about it now, I guess it was because I felt their motives were right.

The reality is: They are just government employees like everyone else. In fact, I have said that to understand prisons, take a DMV office and string barbed wire around it and give the clerks guns. That is the mentality of prisons.

With prosecutors, it is the same way. I think police activity is often driven by the prosecutors, and prosecutors often want to drive up numbers. I will give you two examples of guys I did time with.

One was a fellow named Jerry that had a private plane. And he was offered a quick opportunity to make a lot of money flying drugs into the United States from Mexico. He made one run, made a lot of money, decided he did not want to take that risk any more, he had too much at stake, and he and his wife went into a business making lunches and muffins and then going around to businesses in office buildings and selling them.

Seven years after that one plane flight, one of the guys that was in the drug deal was caught doing something else and the prosecutor said: Can you give us anybody else?

So they gave him Jerry. Jerry was prosecuted and got a 5-year sentence. Now that 5-year sentence did not stop one ounce of drugs from coming into the country. He was out of the business already. But that ran up the score.

The second thing was a fellow named Gordon, a family farmer from, I think he was from Montana, or Idaho. He was from Idaho, and his family farm was in trouble. So he began to grow a little pot and sell it on the side.

A girl that he knew, wasn't dating, but was beaten up by her boyfriend, and he gave her his gun to help protect herself. She was caught doing drugs, and of course the same thing, the prosecutor said: Can you give us anybody else? Oh, yeah, yeah, Gordon.

So she came, set up a deal to buy marijuana from him. At the buy she gave him the gun back. His sentence without the gun would have been a few months in prison. With the gun, it was a mandatory 5-year minimum.

Gordon didn't bring the gun to the buy. The prosecutors instructed the girl to bring it, which then set up the 5-year sentence. Setting up the gun charge did not prevent any more drugs from getting on the street, but it destroyed Gordon and his family.

Those prosecutors were looking for numbers to look like they were tough on crime. It would be better if they were held accountable for how their prosecutions stopped the flow of drugs into our cities.

One last thing. The crack/powder dispute should not be at the Federal level. Crack is sold on the local level on the street because it is chemically unstable and can't be transferred far. It is cooked and sold on the street. That is something the local police can handle.

The Federal Government should be focusing their prosecutions on the people who are transporting huge amounts of cocaine into the country and across State lines. That is where we ought to put our Federal effort, not busting little boutique street markets which sell small amounts of crack on the street.

Senator Casey. I know I am over, but I would just say by way of comment, if we have time before we go, and I will try to ask more, but I really appreciate the focus here on what I will call reentry, the process of leaving prison and how we have not thought nearly enough about it and do not have policies in place to prepare people for the exit into our society, and the numbers on—the number of felons released per day and the idea that we can just release them without any kind of preparation for them and expect them to make it in society.

That is a challenge that I think we have in the Federal Government, and State governments have that challenge as well.

But Senator Webb has the time I have borrowed from him.

> *Senator Webb.* Thank you, Senator Casey.
> I am going to ask another question, but if you care to.
> *Senator Casey.* I think I have to run.
> *Senator Webb.* OK.
> *Senator Casey.* Thank you, very much.
> *Senator Webb.* We appreciate your being here.

I would like to throw something out again that came from the observations that I made when I was looking at the Japanese prison system years ago.

One is, if you were sentenced to 4 or 5 years in a Japanese prison, you had really done something wrong. The sentencing in Japan is very short. They focus on solving a crime. They focus on catching the criminal.

But once the criminal is caught, once the process has gone forward, the length of sentence is not as important as having brought some resolution to the process.

The other thing that they did was they had two different categories of prisons. They did not do this by nature of the severity of a crime. They did it by whether you were a repeat offender.

They had Category A prisons and Category B prisons. I do not know whether they still do this. But a Category A prison was a first offender. Any kind of first offender. And what they did in these prisons, the Category A prisons, is they focused on the prospect of re-entry.

They gave serious skills classes. For instance, at that time, auto repair; today it probably would be computers. But when you got a certificate out of this process, it did not say "Fuchu (phonetic) Prison" on it. It said "Ministry of Labor" on it.

So when someone came out of that system, they had had one bite of the apple, and it was assumed that they were going to re-enter society and they had a productive certificate in their hand.

Then they had Category B prisons. Even if you were convicted of shop lifting five times, you would go to the repeat offender prison and those people made paper bags. They worked. But they did basic, other types of jobs. They were populated very heavily by organized crime, the organized criminals, the aysans (phonetic), and those sorts of things.

But that leads me to two questions. One is, do any of you have an opinion or a belief that length of sentence actually deters crime? I think obviously we do not want to give the wrong impression to people that we are trying to be soft on crime. There are certainly people who deserve to be locked up for a long period of time.

But, (a), does the length of sentence actually deter crime?

And (b), there has to be some other way of looking at a lot of these drug offenses. Let's be honest. Drug use is pandemic in the United States. Would you have thoughts on a different process for people involved in drug crimes, particularly crimes of possession or low-level sales?

Dr. Loury. Yes, I would just say briefly that I think we should repeal mandatory minimum drug laws, and that we should release non-violent drug offenders, or at least mandate treatment for them both within prison and outside.

I mean the point has already been made here that the public safety benefits of locking someone up for non-violent drug offending are de minimis. And the general question that Dr. Jacobson has I think done a good job of articulating of how to efficiently use our limited incarceration resources is raised here.

I mean, it is also raised by Three Strikes' laws that hold people in prison beyond the time in their life cycle when they would be most likely to offend.

The United States, I have heard someone say, is the only country in the world where prison gerontologist is actually an occupational title.

Dr. Jacobson. The deterrence question is a fascinating question, and I am sure we could stay here all day and talk about it. I think most people who look at this stuff would say that the most important deterrent is swift apprehension and punishment.

In fact, the length of time you serve, whether it is 3 years or 6 years for sticking up a 7-11, is something people simply do not make rational calculations about. They don't think about it because they do not know it.

Senator Webb. They don't think about, "Am I going to get caught?"Dr. Jacobson. Correct. And most people do not think they are going to get caught. Most State legislators do not know the length of times for the crimes that they legislate. The public does not know it, although they have some sense that this is illegal; if I do it, I will go to prison; but there is absolutely no evidence that any marginal increase in going from a sentence of 3 to 4, 4 to 6, 8 to 10, or 10 to 20 has any benefit on general deterrence and keeping people from committing crimes—certainly not in relation to how quickly you might get apprehended and punished. Even if the punishment is 10 percent of the sentence.

And to further Dr. Loury's point, it's not just the Three Strikes law, and all these mandatory minimums, which is why we have geriatric prisons. We keep people well beyond their crime-committing years, which does not do any good for specific deterrence. You're not getting anything from keeping that person in prison, and there is no evidence that you get that general deterrence either.

So why we keep people in prison as our prisoners age into their sixties, seventies and eighties, which is happening in almost every State, is an interesting question. It is all about retribution and punishment. And you can understand that at some level if you are the victim or the victim's family of some of the crimes that those people might have committed. But we should just be clear about that discussion.

It is not about public safety. We do not keep people in prison when they are in their sixties, seventies and eighties for public safety. It has absolutely nothing to do with that, and there are huge costs to doing that.

Mr. Nolan. Both Dr. Loury and Dr Jacobson are absolutely right. Prisoners are not rational calculators. They do not think they will get caught. If they thought they would get caught, they would seriously consider the sentences.

Most of the folks I met in prison thought they were smarter than everybody. They never thought they would get caught.

Secondly, because we have scarce resources our system focuses on the broken law. Prison Fellowship supports restorative justice in which you look at the harm done to victims and to the community, and you weigh that. Under restorative justice, the system weighs the relative costs to society of imprisoning an offender, versus the harm they have done. Possessing drugs does not do great harm to society. Shooting a bystander at 7-11 does. That is what the public worries about.

As far as how to deal with drug possession, treatment is so much more effective than incarceration. Dr. Joe Califano, former Secretary of HEW, who is at Columbia University, said: To lock up an addict for 5 years, 10 years, 15 years, but do nothing about their underlying addiction, and then releasing them is a fraud. It is absolutely a fraud on the public.

I also have a suggestion for you, Mr. Chairman. If you could have the staff of this Joint Economic Committee do a study of the economic impact of mass incarceration, one thing is the effect on the economy and the effect on national defense.

With such a huge swath of young men limited in their employability and income after prison—you can see the studies that show that—and impaired with a conviction, they are not able to participate in the economy, buy cars, et cetera, and they also cannot join the military.

Senator Webb. That's one of the principal objectives of this hearing—its economic impact, and we do intend to continue to focus on that.

Mr. Nolan. I just compliment you so much for this.

Senator Webb. Dr. Western?

Dr. Western. So, time served has increased enormously over the last 20 years, so people are serving longer and longer, and estimates attribute about a third of the increase in State and Federal prison populations, to an increase in time served.

And you see this in the penal codes, with a much greater reliance on life sentences. My reading of the research is exactly the same as Dr. Jacobson's. It's not the severity of the sentence that deters, it's the certainty of apprehension, and this is reflected in the effects of the increase in the number of police on the reduction in crime through the 1990s.

That was the big driver of the crime drop, was the very large increase in the number of sworn officers on the street in large urban areas.

On drug possession, through the 1970s and 1980s, I think we can say that drug dealing became a shadow economy, and informal economy in poor neighborhoods, and a context in which there were very few legitimate opportunities, and also in a context in which the problems of drug addiction were becoming more severe.

So we could have treated what was a social and economic problem, in several different ways: We could have used social and economic policy instruments to address the development of this shadow economy in poor neighborhoods, but we chose to adopt a punitive approach that relied heavily on the criminal justice system.

It's not too late to adopt social and economic policy measures to reduce the problems associated with this shadow economy, and I think employment policy and measures for drug treatment have to be significant parts of what an alternative policy approach would look like.

Senator Webb. Thank you. Does anyone else care to comment? [No response.]

Senator Webb. I would like to thank all of you for having taken the time to be with us today. I hope we have begun a process here where we can start shedding the right kind of light on this enormously complicated issue.

On the one hand, I don't think there are any of us who would like to see improper enforcement of the laws. There are people who truly deserve to be in prison.

Again, as I said during my opening statement, we want to be able to break the back of gangs in this country and to deter those types of conduct that can be deterred.

At the same time, I hope, from this hearing, a number of my colleagues and people in the community can understand a little bit better the dynamic that has taken over this issue, which is an unhealthy dynamic for our country.

I intend to continue to focus on this, and I welcome all of your input, not only today, but in the future, to my staff.

We intend to see what we can do to rebalance the scales in this country.

Again, thank you very much for appearing with us today, and we appreciate your testimony very much. This hearing is closed. [Applause.]

[Whereupon, at 12:05 p.m., the hearing was adjourned.]

SUBMISSIONS FOR THE RECORD

Prepared Statement of Senator Jim Webb

I would like to thank Chairman Schumer for agreeing to hold this important hearing and allowing me the opportunity to chair it. I would also like to thank our witnesses for appearing today. Following my remarks, I would ask Vice-Chair Maloney and Senator Brownback to make their opening statements.

Over the course of the period from the mid-1970s until today, the United States has embarked on one of the largest public policy experiments in our history, yet this experiment remains shockingly absent from public debate: the United States now imprisons a higher percentage of its citizens than any other country in the world.

In the name of "getting tough on crime," there are now 2.1 million Americans in federal, state, and local prisons and jails—more people than the populations of New Mexico, West Virginia, or several other states. Compared to our democratic, advanced market economy counterparts, the United States has more people in prison by several orders of magnitude.

All tolled, more than 7 million Americans are under some form of correction supervision, including probation and parole.

America's incarceration rate raises several serious questions. These include: the correlation between mass imprisonment and crime rates, the impact of incarceration on minority communities and women, the economic costs of the prison system, criminal justice policy, and transitioning ex-offenders back into their communities and into productive employment. Equally important, the prison system today calls into question the effects on our society more broadly.

As Winston Churchill noted in 1910, "The mood and temper of the public in regard to the treatment of crime and criminals is one of the most unfailing tests of the civilization of any country." With the world's largest prison population, our prisons test the limits of our democracy and push the boundaries of our moral identity.

The growth in the prison population is only nominally related to crime rates. Just last week in the Washington Post, the deputy director of the Bureau of Justice Statistics stated that "the growth [in the incarceration rate] wasn't really about increase[ed] crime but how we chose to respond to crime."The steep increase in the number of people in prison is driven, according to most experts, by changes in drug policy and tougher sentencing, and not necessarily an increase in crime. Also, the composition of prison admissions has shifted toward less serious offenses: parole violations and drug offenses. Nearly 6 in 10 persons in state prison for a drug offense have no history of violence or significant selling activity. In 2005, four out of five drug arrests were for possession and only one out of five were for sales.

Is incarcerating low-level drug offenders working, particularly given recidivism rates?

The racial composition of America's prisons is alarming. Although African Americans constitute 14 percent of regular drug users, they are 37 percent of those arrested for drug offenses, and 56 percent of persons in state prisons for drug crimes. African Americans serve nearly as much time in federal prisons for drug offenses as whites do for violent crimes.

A black male who does not finish high school now has a 60 percent chance of going to jail. One who has finished high school has a 30 percent chance. We have reached a point where the principal nexus between young African-American men and our society is increasingly the criminal justice system.

Moreover, we are spending enormous amounts of money to maintain the prison system. The combined expenditures of local, state, and federal governments for law enforcement and corrections personnel total over $200 billion. Prison construction and operation has become sought after, if uncertain, tools of economic growth for rural communities.

Are there ways to spend less money, enhance public safety, and make a fairer prison system?

Having such a large prison population also has significant employment and productivity implications. The economic output of prisoners is mostly lost to society while they are imprisoned. These negative productivity effects continue after release. As we've gotten tough on crime, we've given up on rehabilitating offenders.

And we've created additional barriers to reentry with "invisible punishments."These include ineligibility for certain government benefits, such as housing, public assistance, or student loans. It is no longer possible to pay your debt to society.

We want to keep bad people off our streets. We want to break the back of gangs, and we want to cut down on violent behavior. But there's something else going on when we're locking up such a high percentage of our people, marking them at an early age and in many cases eliminating their chances for a productive life as full citizens. It will take years of energy to address these problems. But I am committed to working on a solution that is both responsive to our needs for law and order, and fairer to those ensnared by this system.

I welcome the thoughts of our witnesses today regarding these important topics, and a continuing national dialogue to address these enormous policy issues.

I would like to introduce today's witnesses:

Professor Glenn Loury is the Merton P. Stoltz Professor of the Social Sciences at the Department of Economics at Brown University. He has taught previously at Boston, Harvard and Northwestern Universities, and the University of Michigan. Mr. Loury is a distinguished academic economist who has contributed to a variety of areas in applied microeconomic theory and written on racial inequality.

Professor Bruce Western is the Director of the Multidisciplinary Program in Inequality and Social Policy at the Kennedy School of Government. He taught at Princeton University from 1993 to 2007. Dr. Western's work has focused on the role of incarceration in social and economic inequality in American society. He is the author of Punishment and Inequality in America, a study of the growth and social impact of the American penal system.

Alphonso Albert is the Director of Second Chances, in Norfolk, Virginia, a program designed to provide comprehensive support services that lead to full-time employment and social stability for those individuals impacted by the stigma of being labeled "ex-offender." Prior to working with the Second Chances Program, Mr. Albert served as the Assistant Director and Business Liaison for the City of Norfolk's Enterprise Community initiative, Norfolk Works Inc.

Michael P. Jacobson is the director of the Vera Institute of Justice. He is the author of Downsizing Prisons: How to Reduce Crime and End Mass Incarceration. Prior to joining Vera, he was a professor at the City University of New York Graduate Center and the John Jay College of Criminal Justice. He has served as New York City's Correction Commissioner, Probation Commissioner, and Deputy Budget Director.

Pat Nolan is the Vice-President of Prison Fellowship, where he focuses on efforts to ensure that offenders are better prepared to live healthy, productive, law-abiding lives on their release. He served 15 years in the California State Assembly, four of them as the Assembly Republican Leader. Mr. Nolan has appeared before Congress to testify on matters such as prison work programs, juvenile justice and religious freedom.

Witnesses should please limit their remarks to five minutes, although their entire statements will be entered into the record. After all the witnesses have presented their testimony, we will move to questions.

Prepared Statement of Carolyn Maloney, Vice Chair

Good morning. I would like to thank Chairman Schumer for holding this hearing to examine the economic, political, and social costs of incarceration. I also want to thank Senator Webb for chairing.

The United States has the highest incarceration rates in the world, with more than 2 million Americans currently in jails or prisons. Clearly, imprisonment benefits society and is an important public safety measure. But faced with an unprecedented increase in incarceration, we must ask ourselves whether we are striking the right balance between the costs and benefits of imprisonment.

Putting more resources into creating economic opportunities that provide alternatives to crime would pay dividends in reducing crime and incarceration, while also strengthening families and communities.

We all know that in the long run crime doesn't pay, but it sure is costly. The average annual cost of incarceration for one federal prisoner exceeds $20,000—far more than the average annual cost of $3,700 for a youth program, $6,000 for a job training program or the $13,000 for tuition at public universities.

There is no question that crime rates have dropped in the U.S. over the past decade. Researchers agree that the increase in incarceration rates have been driven by tougher sentences for repeat offenders and drug offenders, mandatory minimums, and a more punitive approach to post-release supervision, rather than an increase in crime.

The racial dimension of incarceration is inescapable. Half of our prison population is African American, yet they represent just 13 percent of the population as a whole. It has become a sad truth that a black man in his late twenties without a high school diploma is more likely to be in jail than to be working. The effect on black communities has been devastating.

As noted Harvard sociologist Orlando Patterson wrote in the New York Times recently, one in three African American males in their 30s now has a prison record. He somberly noted, "These numbers and rates are incomparably greater than anything achieved at the height of the Jim Crow era."Women are typically convicted of nonviolent offenses. Most women who enter the criminal justice system have experienced physical or sexual abuse, and many have physical or mental health problems. These inmates may actually benefit from alternatives to imprisonment, such as suspended sentences coupled with extensive counseling.

When mothers are incarcerated, their children may be placed in foster care, or with other family members who then need financial assistance to provide for the children. Moreover, the removal of a significant family member can affect the healthy development of children.

The Catholic Charities Diocese of Brooklyn and Queens operate a week-long summer camp that provides opportunities for incarcerated mothers to have quality time with their children. Such programs serve as a means to maintain family bonds, and possibly provide a smoother transition and resumption of parental responsibilities upon release. If this program shows success, it could serve as a model for the nation.

Providing employment and training assistance for ex-offenders is critical to reducing barriers to employment, and it benefits families. I support the Second Chance Act of 2007, which provides grants for re-entry programs that provide mentoring, academic and vocation education, and employment assistance, and substance abuse treatment for ex-offenders.

I look forward to hearing from our distinguished panel about how best to protect public safety, while addressing the many costs of imprisonment.

JOINT ECONOMIC COMMITTEE SENATE REPUBLICANS SENATOR SAM BROWNBACK, SENIOR REPUBLICAN SENATOR

Mr. Chairman, thank you for holding this important hearing regarding "Mass Incarceration in the Unites States: At What Cost?''

As you know, for some time, I, along with my colleagues on the judiciary committee, have been working extremely hard to enact legislation that will have a positive effect upon our prison system, the Recidivism Reduction and Second Chance Act of 2007. It goes without saying that we have a broken prison system—and the results are devastating not only to those incarcerated and their families but to society as a whole.

This year alone, more than 650,000 inmates will be released from prison, and studies show that approximately two-thirds will likely be rearrested within three years of release.

The economic effects of our broken system are staggering and leave our state and local governments financially vulnerable.

State corrections systems across the country have experienced tremendous growth since 1980. Between 1980 and 2005, the total number of adults under corrections supervision (prisons, jails, probation, and parole) increased 283 percent from approximately 2 million in 1980 to more than 7 million in 2005. Likewise, state spending on corrections has grown faster than nearly any other state budget item—increasing from $9 billion in 1984 to $41 billion in 2004.

A recent report from the Pew Charitable Trusts revealed that the Nation's prison population is projected to grow an additional 13 percent over the next five years. State and federal prison populations are expected to add approximately 192,000 persons at a cost of $27.5 billion between 2006 and 2011.

It is time that we fix this broken system. It is time that we invest federal dollars wisely on programs that are successful in reducing the rates of recidivism for the program participants.

For too long, we have stood back and watched this situation deteriorate. I am pleased that there are States, such as Kansas, that are leading the way in innovative reentry programs with great success.

In 2007, the Kansas prison population was projected to grow 26 percent by 2016 at a cost to taxpayers of $500 million in additional construction and operating costs. High rates of failure among people on community supervision and low rates of in- prison program completion were identified as key factors driving the growth.

During the 2007 Session, Kansas policymakers overwhelmingly enacted a legislative package that is expected to avert the need to build nearly 1,300 new prison beds and to save the state $80 million over the next five years.

Mr. Chairman, we need to encourage such innovation and build upon the experiences of States such as Kansas in order to reduce crime and re-arrest and incarceration rates.

Although States have taken the first step in designing strategies to avert growth in their prison populations and corrections expenditures, they will need the support of the federal government going forward.

The role of the federal government in state and local re-entry must be limited, but can still have a significant impact.

I am pleased that our federal agencies have taken the lead and are collaborating on programs designed to increase public safety while providing services to inmates, which will, in turn, decrease recidivism.

Through legislation such as the Recidivism Reduction and Second Chance Act of 2007, small amounts of federal dollars can help to encourage innovation in re-entry, reduce recidivism and establish standards of performance.

In addition to the public response, organizations such as Prison Fellowship Ministries have led the way in providing non-profit assistance and I am pleased the Pat Nolan, Vice-President of Prison Fellowship Ministries is joining us today. These organizations are doing wonderful work in treating the "whole person"—this is beneficial to both inmates and their families and has transformed the lives of those who are incarcerated.

However, we must not stop here. We must continue to move toward rectifying the recidivism rates in this country.

Additionally, family environments need to be improved so that children are brought up under more stable conditions. Children who come from fatherless homes are 20 times more likely to be incarcerated and children who do not graduate high school are 3.5 times more likely to be incarcerated.

We can no longer set idly by and watch while ex-offenders and their families deteriorate—especially the children of those incarcerated—which not only leads to hardships for the ex-offenders and their families, but to society as a whole.

We must support programs that provide public safety, reduce the cost of recidivism on States, and provide for a second chance for ex-offenders and their families. I look forward to hearing the statements from today's witnesses.

PREPARED STATEMENT OF CONGRESSMAN ROBERT C. "BOBBY" SCOTT, CHAIRMAN FOR THE SUBCOMMITTEE ON CRIME, TERRORISM, AND HOMELAND SECURITY

Thank you, Mr. Chairman. And thank you, Chairman Webb and Vice Chairwoman Maloney for the opportunity to be with you today as we discuss this very important subject of the cost of the mass incarceration we have in the United States. Today, the U.S. is the world's leading incarcerator, by far, with an average incarceration rate over 7 times the international average. The average incarceration rate in the rest of the world is about 100 per 100,000 citizens. The rate in the U.S. is over 700 per 100,000 residents, and in some inner-city communities, the rate goes over 4,000 per 100,000. Russia is the next closest in rate of incarceration with 611 per 100,000 citizens. Everybody else is much below, such as India, the world's largest Democracy, with 30 per 100,000 and China, the world's largest country by population, with a rate 118 per 100,000.

We didn't get to this position overnight. I have learned that when it comes to crime policy, you have a choice—you can reduce crime or you can play politics. The politics of crime call for so-called "tough on crime" approaches such as more life without parole, mandatory minimum sentences, and treating more juveniles as adults or gang members. Under the get tough approach, no matter how tough you were last year, you have to get tougher this year. We have been getting tougher year-by-year for over 30 years now. Since 1970, we have gone from around 300,000 persons incarcerated in the U.S. to over 2 million, and annual prison costs now are over $65 billion this year.

And the U.S. has some of the world's most severe punishments for crime, including for juveniles. Of the more than 2200 juveniles sentenced to life without parole, all but 12 are in the U.S.

Research and analysis, as well as common sense, tell us that no matter how tough you are on the people you prosecute for crime today, unless you are addressing the reasons they got to the point to commit the crimes in the first place, the next wave developing in the system will simply replace the ones you take out and crime continues. This is not to say that we shouldn't prosecute crimes or that imprisonment has no impact. The problem is that you reach the point of diminishing returns in a particular case with no appreciable benefit. In fact, you run the risk of it diminishing returns to the point of actually being counterproductive, such as when you have so many in a neighborhood with criminal records that a criminal record no longer represents a stigma or provides an effective deterrent to crime.

A corollary cost of the mass incarceration resulting from "tough on crime' politics is the fact that it falls in a grossly disproportionate manner on minorities, particularly Black and Hispanic youth. The sad reality is that many children born in minority communities today are, from birth, without an appropriate intervention, on a "cradle to prison pipeline". When we see how simple it is to get them on a "cradle to college pipeline", it is tragic, and much more costly to society, economically and socially, if we don't do so. There are also other costs to consider when crime rates are high, such as the medical costs associated with gun crimes. One study estimated the annual cost of gun violence in the U.S. to be $100 billion.

Fortunately, we have a choice. All the credible research and evidence shows that a continuum of evidenced-based programs for youth identified as being at risk of involvement in delinquent behavior, and those already involved, will not only put kids on an appropriate "pipeline", but will save much more than they cost when compared to the avoided law enforcement, prison and other costs. Washington State did an extensive study showing that evidenced-based prevention and rehabilitation programs reduce crime and save money when compared to waiting for crimes to be committed and sending offenders to prison. Washington State adopted many of these initiatives and consequently has avoided the necessity of building new, expensive prisons. The question is whether we have the political will to make that choice.

Washington made that choice, adopted the policy, avoided building more prisons, and reduced crime at the same time.

There is also a huge opportunity cost to not doing what research and evidence says will reduce crime. To illustrate, let's examine the impact in Virginia of the lost opportunities associated with the tough on crime sound byte "abolish parole". Rather than invest in proven crime reduction measures that work, Virginia chose to go down the costly and wasteful path of abolishing parole. Despite the proponents claim, even if it worked perfectly, the reduction in violent crime would be a statistically insignificant 3 percent, and even that would be without considering the counterproductive effects of no parole, such as the fact that you can't hold hardened criminals longer and the loss of an incentive for prisoners to get an education and job training while in prison. They estimated the cost of abolishing parole was $2.2 billion to build new prisons and about a billion in annual operating costs. Doing some back of the envelope arithmetics, let's see what we can do with that kind of money. There are 11 Congressional districts in Virginia, so that's about $200 million for construction and about $90 million for operations per Congressional district of 600,000 people. So for a city of around 100,000, you're talking about more than $30 million for construction and $15 million operating.

Alternatively, here's what you could do with that kind of money in a small city:

Construction:	
10—$3 million Boys and Girls Clubs or family resource center	30M
Operating:	
10 clubs or centers @ $600,000/yr .	6M
1,000 summer jobs @ $1,000	1M
1,000 summer camp scholarships @ $1,000	1M
4,000 after school programs @ $250	1M
2,000 college scholarships @ $2,000	4M
Services for 200 juveniles @ $10,000/year	2M

So you can spend money codifying a slogan without knowing whether you are reducing or increasing crime or you can spend the same amount of money, or even less, on evidenced-based prevention programs and rehabilitation programs proven to reduce crime.

Of course, having so many people locked up, we are now seeing a huge number returning to our communities, in most cases no better off then when they left and, in all too many cases, much worse. This year, more than 650,000 people will be released from state and federal prisons, along with more than 9 million people leaving local jails.

According to the Department of Justice's Bureau of Justice Statistics, some 67 percent of offenders leaving state and federal prison are rearrested within three years. Most offenders go into prison unskilled, poorly educated, and poorly motivated and over one-third of all jail inmates have some physical or mental disability.

With no parole, no good conduct credits or other self-development incentives, limited vocational or other development programs in prison, and all the disqualifications that result from a felony record, it is not hard to see why the recidivism rate is so high.

One program in the federal prison system that has proven to be a huge incentive program for not only good conduct and safer, easier to manage prisons, and getting an education required to qualify for it, but has also for developing work skills proven to increase employment after release and reduce crime, is the Federal Prison Industries, or FPI program. Unfortunately, a provision in the just passed Senate Defense Authorization bill essentially guts the FPI program.

The Second Chance Act now pending before the Congress provides a host of evidenced-based approaches designed to reduce the high rate of recidivism now occurring.

If we are going to continue to send more and more people to prison with longer and longer sentences, we should do as much as we reasonably can to assure that when they do return they don't go back to prison due to new crimes. The primary reason for doing so is not to benefit offenders, although it does—the primary reason for doing so is to better assure that all of us and other members of the public will not be victims of crime due to recidivism and to save the high cost of law enforcement and incarceration.

Again, Mr. Chairman, I would like to thank you for holding this very important hearing and for inviting me to sit with you for it. Thank you.

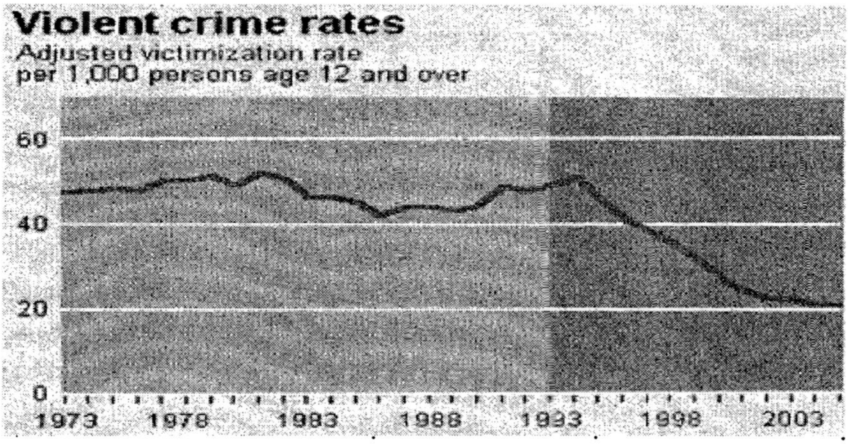

PREPARED STATEMENT OF GLENN C. LOURY, MERTON P. STOLTZ PROFESSOR OF THE SOCIAL SCIENCES, DEPARTMENT OF ECONOMICS, BROWN UNIVERSITY

Mass Incarceration and American Values

Mr. Chairman, Madam Vice-Chairwoman, and distinguished Members, I thank you for the opportunity to address this vital issue before your committee.

There are six main points about the advent of mass incarceration as a crime control policy in the United States that I wish to make with this testimony:

1. First, I wish to emphasize that with the advent of the mass incarceration policy we have witnessed an historic expansion of coercive state power, deployed internally on a massive scale. Violent crime peaked in the early 1990s, and began what has proven to be a long, precipitous decline. (See the Figure below. A similar trend applies for non-violent property crimes.) But, no one saw this coming. Crime was a real problem two decades ago, and fighting a war on crime was bipartisan national policy.

As a result of this policy, the American prison system has grown into a leviathan unmatched in human history. Never has a supposedly "free country" denied basic liberty to so many of its citizens. As of December 2006, some two-and-one-quarter million persons were being held in the nearly 5,000 prisons and jails that are scattered, like an archipelago, across America's urban and rural landscapes. Incarceration is now being used in the United States on an unprecedented scale. We imprison at a far higher rate than any other industrial democracy in the world. We imprison at a higher rate than Russia or China, and vastly more than any of the countries in Europe.

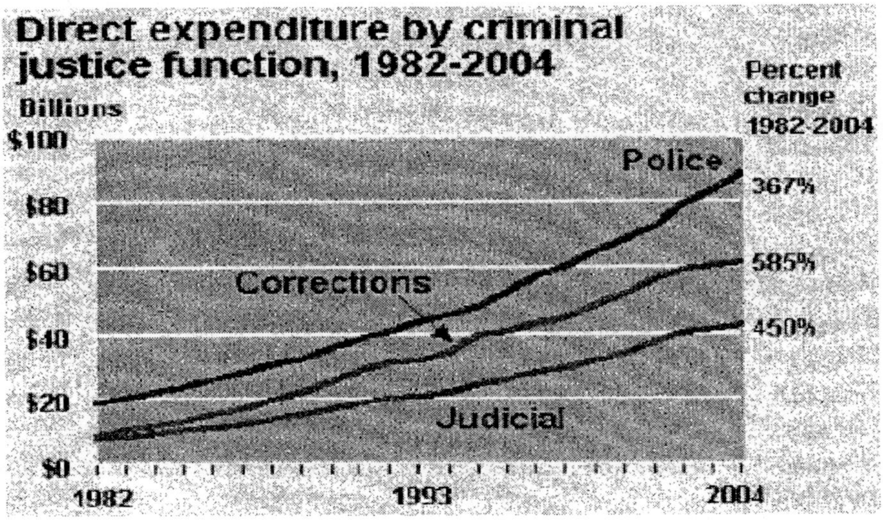

And, it is costing us a veritable fortune. Spending on law enforcement and corrections at all levels of government now totals roughly a fifth of a trillion dollars per year. In constant dollars, this spending has more than quadrupled over the last quarter-century. The table below indicates how this spending breaks-down by function:

2. *Second*, I claim that this high level of imprisonment is not any longer, if ever it was, a rational response to high levels of crime. Rather, our mass incarceration policy is an historical inheritance, bequeathed to us by wave after wave of crime- fighting at the state and the federal levels over the past 35 years. This policy response, I firmly believe, has now become counter-productive. (The so-called War on Drugs, about which I have more to say at the end of this testimony, is a leading example of one such misconceived policy initiative that now has us in its grip.)

3. *Third,* I wish to point out that institutional arrangements for dealing with criminal offenders in the United States have evolved to serve expressive as well as instrumental ends. We have wanted to "send a message"—to the criminals and to the law-abiding public, alike—and, have done so with a vengeance. In the process, we have answered the question: Who is to blame for the maladies which beset our troubled civilization? We have, in effect, constructed a national narrative. We have created scapegoats, indulged our need to feel virtuous about

ourselves, and assuaged our fears. We have met the enemy, and the enemy is THEM—the violent, predatory, immoral, irredeemable "thugs." I believe that this narrative, which supports and encourages our embrace of the policy of mass incarceration is, itself, a sociologically naive and morally superficial view.

4. Fourth, I wish to observe that these people who have offended against our laws are nevertheless human beings. And, while they may deserve punishment, imprisoning them is something that We the People of the United States of America are doing. Indeed, punishment is one of the most politically salient things that we do in a democracy: the state is forcibly depriving citizens of their liberty. And, while this practice is necessary for the maintenance of order in society, it should always be done humanely, in a manner that comports with our deepest political values. We ought never to lose sight of the essential humanity of those whom we punish—and, of the humanity of those to whom offenders are connected via intimate ties of social and psychic affiliation. Unfortunately, we have not always lived up to this high standard. Thus, Confronting Confinement, a report released last year from the Commission on Safety and Abuse in America's Prisons (of which former US Attorney General Nicholas Katzenback was co-chairman), found that our penal institutions are (i) dangerously overcrowded, that (ii) they rely overly much on physical isolation to manage the behavior of inmates (a practice which, the Commission found can have a lasting adverse effect on the prisoners' mental health), and that they are horribly, unnecessarily violent. The report estimates that more than 1.5 million people annually are released from prisons and jails with a life-threatening infectious disease—the HIll, drug-resistant staph infections, hepatitis-C, and tuberculosis; and, that at least one out of every six prisoners—over 350,000 people on a given day—are "seriously mentally ill."

5. Fifth, I must call attention to a huge gap between the races in the incidence of punishment which exists in our country. Black Americans and Hispanics together account for about one-quarter of the overall national population, but constitute about two-thirds of state and federal prison populations. The extent of racial disparity in imprisonment rates is greater than in any other major arena of American social life: at eight-to-one, the black-white ratio of incarceration rates dwarfs the two-to-one ratio of unemployment rates, three-to-one non-marital child bearing ratio, the two-to-one black-white ratio of infant mortality rates and one-to-five ratio of net worth. As the table below makes clear, more black male high school dropouts are incarcerated than belong to unions or are enrolled in all government social welfare programs, combined.

Men Incarcerated (2000), in Unions, or in Social Programs (1996)

	Whites	Hispanics	Blacks
All men, age 20 to 40			
In prison or jail	1.60%	4.60%	11.50%
In labor union	9.70%	10.70%	11.50%
On welfare	1.70%	1.40%	2.30%
In any program (including welfare) .	6.70%	4.90%	10.80%
Male high school dropouts, age 20 to 40			
In prison or jail	6.70%	6.00%	32.40%
In labor union	6.30%	8.10%	2.30%
On welfare	6.20%	1.70%	3.70%
In any program (including welfare)	17.90%	6.30%	24.00%

* Survey of Incomes and Program Participation (1996).

The scandalous fact of the matter is that the primary contact between poorly educated black American men of a certain age and the American state is via the police and the penal apparatus. For instance, among black male high school dropouts ages 20 to 40, a third were under lock and key on a given day in the year 2000, while fewer than 3 percent belonged to a union, and less than one-quarter were enrolled in any kind of social program (according to Harvard University sociologist, Bruce Western.) The coercive aspect of government is the most salient feature of their experience of the public sector. Western estimates that some 58 percent of black male dropouts born between 1965 and 1969 were sent to prison on a felony offense at least once before reaching the age of 35.

For these men, and the families and communities with which they are associated, the adverse effects of incarceration will extend beyond their stays behind bars. To see how the post-1980 prison boom affected Americans differently, depending on their race and their social class, consider two birth cohorts of black and white men. The first cohort was born in 1945 to 1949, just after World War II.

These individuals reached their mid-thirties by 1970, just before the rapid increase in imprisonment rates. The second cohort was born during the Vietnam War, from 1965 to 1969, and reached their mid-thirties during the height of the prison boom. The table below compares the imprisonment experience of these two cohorts, broken down by race and level of education:

Cumulative Risk of Imprisonment

	All	Less than HS	HS or GED	All Noncollege	Some College
	(1)	(2)	(3)	(4)	(5)
White men					
Born 1945 to 1949	1.4	4	1	2.1	0.5
Born 1965 to 1969	2.9	11.2	3.6	5.3	0.7
Black men					
Born 1945 to 1949	10.5	17.1	6.5	12	5.9
Born 1965 to 1969	20.5	58.9	18.4	30.2	4.9

Notice that the aggregate risk of imprisonment is twice as great in the later cohort—2.9 percent as compared to 1.4 percent for white men; and, 20.5 percent as compared to 10.5 percent for black men. Moreover, one can see from the table that the experience of incarceration for poorly educated black men is estimated to be four times more prevalent in the later than in the earlier cohort—58.9 percent as compared to 17.1 percent. The massive scale of this policy shift is stunning. To repeat: there is a nearly three-fifths chance that a black male with less than HS diploma born between 1965–69 will have gone to prison or jail at least once prior to reaching age 35.

Table 5.2. Wages, Employment, Earnings

	Incarceration Status		
	Never	Before	After
Hourly wages (dollars per hour)			
White	14.7	11.14	11.8
Hispanic	13.59	12.3	10.31
Black	12.34	10.25	9.25
Annual employment (weeks per year)			
White	44	37	23
Hispanic	43	35	24
Black	40	35	21
Annual earnings (thousands of dollars per year)			
White	26.44	13.7	9.76
Hispanic	23.9	13.29	9.14
Black	20.37	13.34	7.02

A fundamental point to bear in mind is that the experience of prison feeds-back to affect the life course of those incarcerated in an adverse manner. The vast majority of inmates return to society. The evidence that prison adversely affects the subsequent life chances of the incarcerated is considerable and impressive.

The table above reproduces Harvard University sociologist Bruce Western's (admittedly crude but suggestive) estimates of the impact of imprisonment on subsequent labor market outcomes. Hourly wages of incarcerated black men are 10 percent lower after prison than before. And weeks worked per year of all imprisoned men are down by 1⁄3 or more after release, as compared with prior to their incarceration. Now, consider the nearly 60 percent of black male high school dropouts born in the late 1960s who will have been imprisoned before their fortieth year. For these men, their links to family have been disrupted; their subsequent work lives will be diminished; their voting rights are often permanently revoked. They will suffer, quite literally, a "civic excommunication" from American democracy. It is no exaggeration to say that, given our zeal for social discipline, these men will be consigned to a permanent, non-white, male nether caste. And yet, since these men—whatever their shortcomings—have emotional and sexual and family needs, including the need to be fathers and lovers and husbands—we will have created a bio-political situation where the children of this nether caste are likely themselves to join a new generation of untouchables.

A central reality of our time is the fact that there has opened a wide racial gap in the acquisition of cognitive skills, the extent of law-abidingness, the stability of family relations, the attachment to the work force, and the like. This disparity in human development is, as a historical matter, rooted in political, economic, social, and cultural factors peculiar to this society and reflective of its unlovely racial history: it is a societal, not communal or personal, achievement. At the level of the individual case we must, of course, act as if this were not so. There could be no law, no civilization, without the imputation to particular persons of responsibility for their wrongful acts. But the sum of a million cases, each one rightly judged on its merits to be individually fair, may nevertheless constitute a great historic wrong. The state does not only deal with individual cases. It also makes policies in the aggregate, and the consequences of these policies are more or less knowable. And who can honestly say—who can look in the mirror and say with a straight face—that we now have laws and policies that we would endorse if we did not know our own situation and genuinely considered the possibility that we might be the least advantaged?

6. Finally, I would like to make a few observations about the so-called War on Drugs. This policy has not been successful in my view, and it has had a hugely disparate, adverse impact on the African American community. Consider the table below, showing the trend in drug arrest rates by race since 1970.

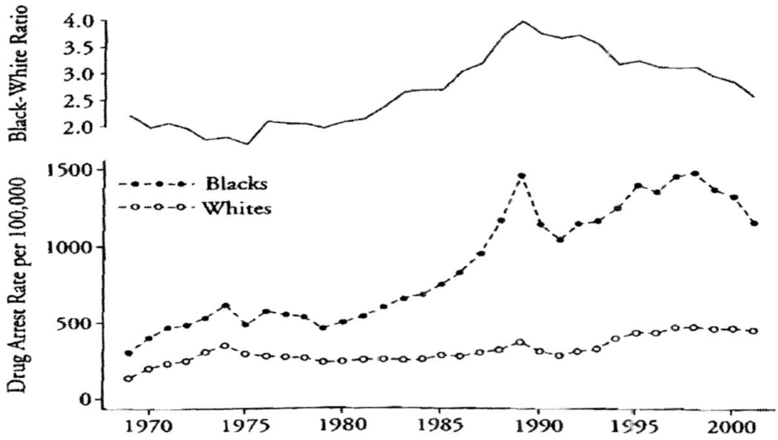

Figure 2.2. Drug Offers and Arrest Rate Ratio.

Drug Arrests of Blacks Spike in Late 80's

Blacks were twice as likely as whites to be arrested for a drug offense in 1975, but four-times as likely (1,460 versus 365 per 100,000) by 1989. For all of the 1990s, drug arrest rates remained at historically unprecedented levels. Yet, according to the National Survey on Drug Abuse (NSDA), drug use among adults fell from 20 percent in 1979 to 11 percent in 2000. A similar trend occurred for adolescents.

In the age groups 12–17 and 18–25, usage of marijuana, cocaine and heroin all peaked at roughly the same time (in the late 1970s), and began a steady decline thereafter (Tonry 2004, Figure 5.14, p. 132). Thus, a decline in drug use across the board had begun a decade before the War on Drugs was initiated.

There are some interesting discrepancies between the racial gap in drug use and in drug arrests. In figure 2.2 (above) one can see that the drug arrest rate for blacks stood at twice the rate for whites in the late 1970s, rising to 4 times the white rate by 1990.

On the other hand, figure 2.3 (below) reveals that throughout this period white high school seniors reported using drugs at a significantly higher rate than blacks.

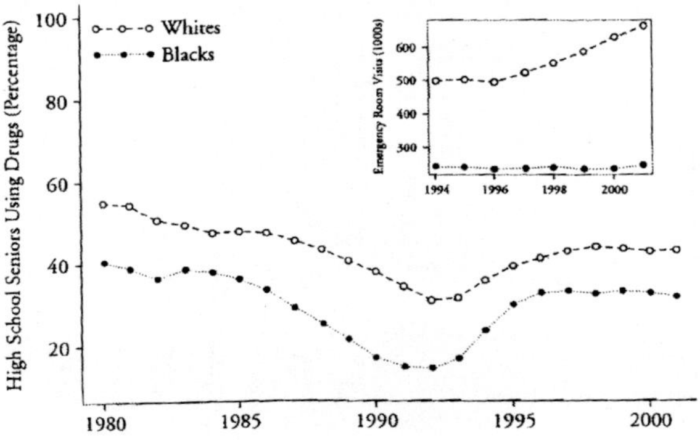

Figure 2.3. High School Seniors Reporting Drug Use.

Presumably this relatively high rate of drug use in the early 80's in the mainstream of American society partially explains the urgency many felt to mount a national attack on the problem. Yet, how successful has the effort been, and at what cost?

As the data below make clear, retail prices on the street of illicit drugs fell steadily and sharply throughout the period 1980–2000 (with the exception of meth- amphetamine which experienced a price spike in the late 80's–early 90's), even as "war mobilization" caused drug incarceration rate to skyrocket:

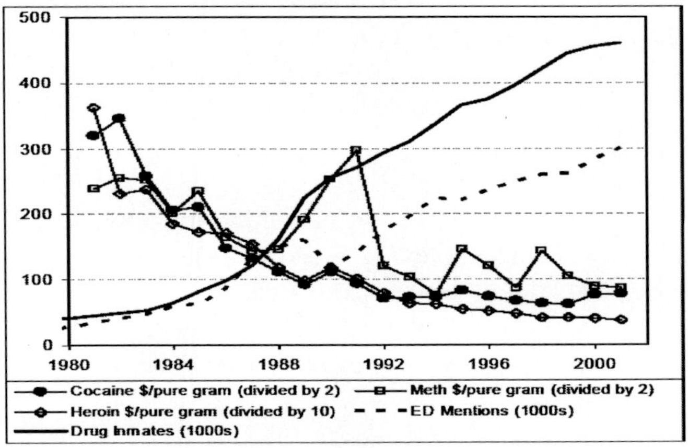

Source: Caulkins, Reuter and Taylor, "Can Supply Restrictions Lower Price?" Contributions to Economic Analysis and Policy Vol. 5 (2006).

Winning the War? Drug Prices, Emergency Treatment and Icarceration Rates: 1980-2000.

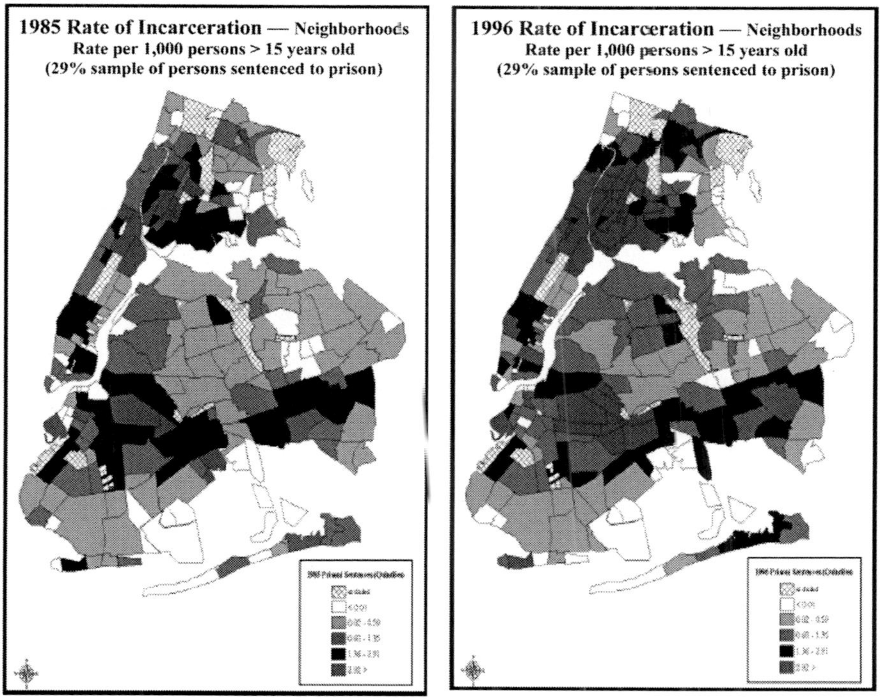

Source: Fagan, West and Holland, "Reciprocal Effects of Crime and Incarceration in New York City Neighborhoods." Fordham Urban Law Journal, 2003.

Changes in the spatial concentration of incarceration in New York City 1985-1996.

SPATIAL EFFECTS

What all this comes to is that, to save "our" middle class kids from the threat of their being engulfed by a drug epidemic that might not have even existed by the time drug incarceration began rapidly rising in the 1980s, we criminalized "our"underclass kids. Arrests went up and up, drug prices went down and down, and drug consumptions seems not to have been much impacted by the policy.

An interesting case in point is New York City. Columbia University criminologist Jeffery Fagan and his colleagues have analyzed data on arrests in various New York City residential neighborhoods and police precincts. They report that, 70 percent of state inmates in New York come from New York City. Between 1990 and 2003 the number of state prison inmates coming from the city rose from 55,000 to 70,000. The City also had an average daily jail population of nearly 18,000 in 1999. "Rates of incarceration in NYC have been largely unaffected by the city's dramatic declines in crime. Moreover, the increase in incarceration is in part "attributable to aggressive enforcement of drug laws, especially street-level enforcement resulting in large numbers of felony arrests of retail drug sellers." They note that "drug-related offenses have accounted for an increasing proportion of prison admissions—up from 12 percent of state prison admissions in 1985 to 31 percent in 1990, to 38 percent in 1996. Some 11,600 residents of NYC entered the NY state prison system on drug- related offenses in 1996, compared to 9,345 in 1990.

As the maps above make clear, incarceration was highest in the City's poorest neighborhoods though these were not in every instance the neighborhoods where crime rates were highest. Most interestingly, when these data were analyzed at the level of police precincts, the authors discovered a perverse positive feedback of incarceration on crime: higher incarceration in a given neighborhood seemed to predict higher crime rates one year later in that same neighborhood. They concluded that the growth and persistence of incarceration over time were due primarily to drug enforcement and to sentencing laws that require imprisonment for repeat felons. Police scrutiny was more intensive and less forgiving in neighborhoods high incarceration neighborhoods, and parolees returning to such neighborhoods were more closely monitored. This discretionary, spatially discriminatory police behavior led to a high and increasing rate of repeat prison admissions in the designated neighborhoods, even as crime rates fell.

Further evidence along these lines can be found by examining the experience of anti-marijuana law enforcement. Comprehensive data on this have been collected for New York City by the Queens College sociologist Harry Levine and his colleagues, and are presented in the tables that follow. These data speak volumes about the racially discriminatory and spatially selective enforcement of anti-drug statutes. Bear in mind when viewing these data that U.S. Government statistics have consistently found that White teenagers and young adults use marijuana as much, or more, than Blacks and Hispanics do. Nonetheless, in 2006 in New York City, the per capita arrest rate of Blacks was nearly 8 times the rate of Whites. Again, I wish to express my gratitude to the Committee for this opportunity to present my reflections on this urgent matter of national policy.

Responses by Dr. Glenn C. Loury to Questions from Representative Robert C. "Bobby" Scott

Question 1. In your testimony, you state that high levels of imprisonment have become counterproductive. Please elaborate.

Response. The three main reasons that I see the current high level of imprisonment as being counterproductive are as follows:

1. Holding people in prison doesn't make them "better." Rather, it makes them "worse." Not only do we fail to rehabilitate criminals when they're in custody. Incarceration has a significant adverse impact on the employability (weeks work down by a third) and the earnings (wages off by 10 percent) of ex-convicts. They are "scarred" by the experience of prison. Their mental and physical health is negatively affected. Recidivism rates are such that nearly 50 percent of prisoners are returned to custody within three years of their release.
2. The amount of public safety "purchased" for society by using prisons on the scale that we are now using them does not justify the cost incurred to hold prisoner behind bars, let alone the cost we're imposing on prisoners and the communities from which they come.

The economist, Steven Levitt, estimates that more money spent on policing, and less on imprisonment, would lead to lower crime rates (Journal of Economic Perspectives, 2004). The conservative political scientist, John Dilulio, opined in the Wall Street Journal nearly a decade ago (March 12, 1999) that we were then overusing prison for crime control purposes, and that we should aim toward "zero- growth in incarceration." Some "tough on crime" policies, like "three strikes and you're out" hold offenders behind bars for decades beyond the point in the lifecycle after which people cease to be a threat to society. Given the widespread problems of over-crowding and the huge pressure on state budgets due to the cost of running these mammoth prison systems, cell space devoted to holding non-violent drug offenders could be much more effectively utilized.

3. Imprisonment on the scale which we are now undertaking, and that is so concentrated among the poorly educated, urban, racial minority male youth populations of our country, does not make the communities from which offenders are taken better, it makes them worse. A number of observers (see, for example, Fagan et al., "Reciprocal effects of crime and incarceration in New York City Neighborhoods,"Fordham Law Journal 2003) have noted that massive and spatially concentrated incarceration feeds-back to have a detrimental effect on the social climate in the communities to which inmates inevitably return. The legitimacy of law enforcement is weakened; the moral norms against offending are undermined; the stigma of imprisonment is eviscerated; the intensity of

law enforcement scrutiny is enhanced. Fagan et al. actually find that New York City neighborhoods which experienced the highest rates of incarceration in one year were, other things equal, likely to experience higher rates of crime in future years.

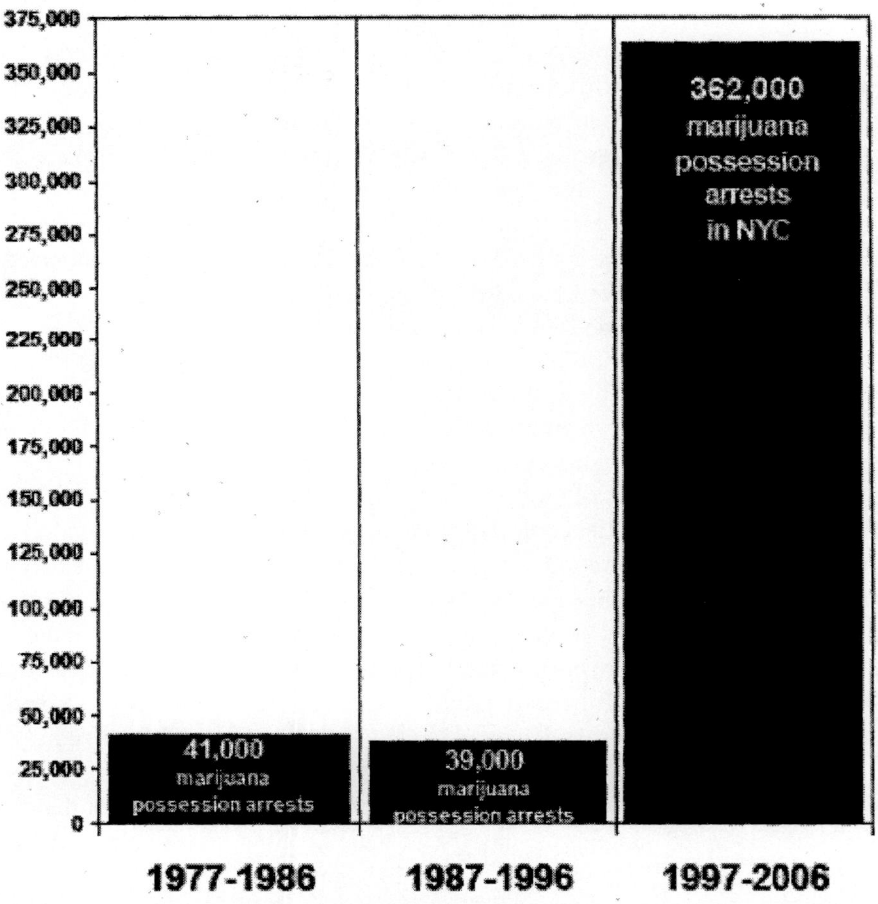

Source: New York State Dvision of Criminal Justice services, Computize Criminal History system. Includes all fingerprintable arrests for NY State Penal Law Article 221 offenses as the most serious charge in an arrest event. Ages 16 and older. 1978 data was used for 1977.

1. Marijuana Possession Arrests in New York City in Three Decades.

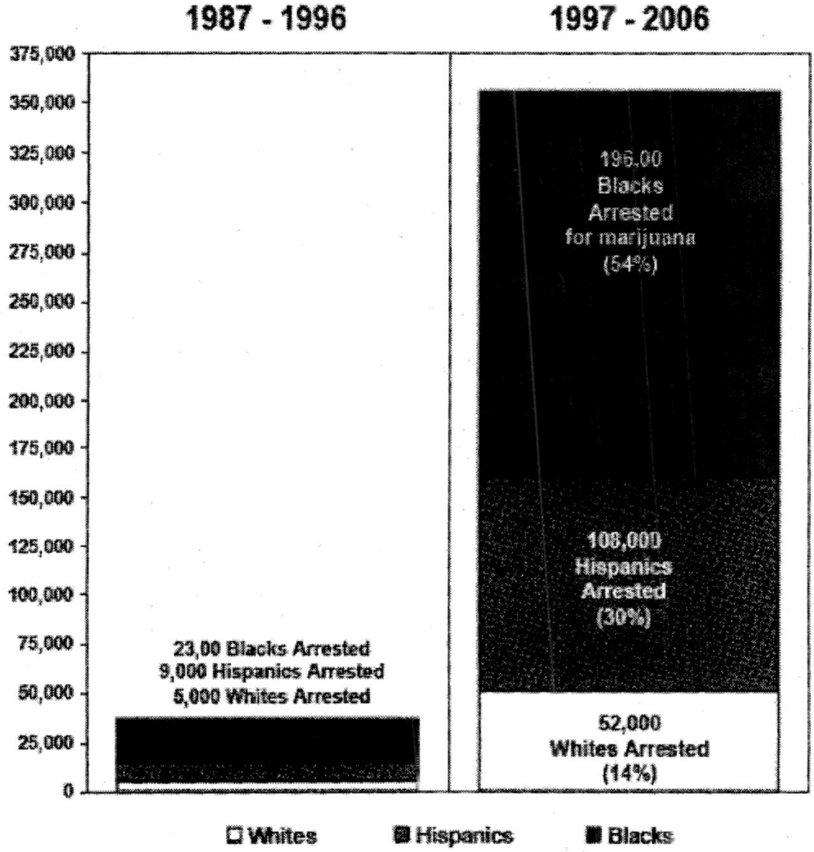

Source: New York Stare Division of Crimilal Justice services, Computize Criminal History system. Includes all fingerprintable arrests for NY State Penal Law Article 221 offenses as the most serious charge in an arrest event. Ages 16 and older.

2. New York City Marijuana Posseion Arresrs of Whites, Hispanics and Blacks in two decades.

PREPARED STATEMENT OF BRUCE WESTERN, DIRECTOR, DEPARTMENT OF SOCIOLOGY, HARVARD UNIVERSITY

Mr Chairman and Members of the Committee: thank you for the opportunity of testifying today about the causes and economic effects of the growth in the incarceration rate.

I. Trends in Incarceration

The fraction of the population in state and federal prison has increased in every single year for the last 34 years. The rate of imprisonment today is now five times higher than in 1972 [1]. The US rate of imprisonment is five to ten times higher than in the longstanding democracies of Western Europe, and is only rivaled, though not exceeded, by the incarceration rates of South Africa and Russia.

Today's novel rates of incarceration are most remarkable for their concentration among young African American men with little schooling. While fewer than 2 percent of young white men, aged 22 to 30, were in prison or jail in 2004, the incarceration rate of young black men was 13.5 percent (Table 1). Among young black men who had never been to college, 21.1 percent were locked up on an average day in 2004. At the bottom of the education ladder, I estimate that more than 1 in 3 black male high school dropouts were incarcerated in 2004.

To examine the chances of going to prison over a lifetime, I also calculated the percentage of men who have ever been to prison by their mid-thirties. (Most prisoners will be admitted for the first time before age 35.) These percentages describe the prevalence of imprisonment, not jail incarceration—at least 12 months in a state or federal facility, and an average of 34 months of time served. For men born in the late 1940s who reached their mid-thirties in 1979, blacks were 9 percent likely to go to prison.

Table 1. Incarceration rates for young men, 1980 and 2004

	Whites		Blacks	
	1980	2004	1980	2004
Men Aged 22–30 in Prison or Jail (%)				
All men .	0.6	1.9	5.7	13.5
Without College Education	1.1	4.2	7.4	21.1
High School Dropouts	2.3	7.3	11.7	34.2
Men with Prison Records by Age 34 (%)				
All men	1.2	2.8	9.0	22.8
Without College Education	1.8	5.1	12.1	30.9
High School Dropouts	4.2	14.8	14.7	62.5

Note: Percentage of men with prison records are risks of imprisonment estimated for birth cohorts born 1945–1949 by 1979, and 1970–1974 by 2004. Sources and methods are described in Western (2006).

For black men born in the late 1960s, the lifetime chances of imprisonment had grown to 22.8 percent. Among black men without college education now in their early forties, nearly a third have prison records. For young black male dropouts, prison time has become a normal life event, affecting 60 percent of those born since the late 1960s. Young black men are now more likely to go to prison than to graduate college with a 4-year degree, or to serve in the military [2].

These extraordinary rates of incarceration are new. We need only go back 20 years to find a time when the penal system was not pervasive in the lives of young African American men.

In the period of mass incarceration, blacks have remained 7 to 8 times more likely to be incarcerated than whites. The large black-white disparity in incarceration is unmatched by most other social indicators. Racial disparities in unemployment (2 to 1), nonmarital childbearing (3 to 1), infant mortality (2 to 1), and wealth (1 to 5) are all significantly lower than the 7 to 1 black-white ratio in incarceration rates [3].

II. Invisible Disadvantage

Because of high incarceration rates, conventional measures of economic well-being are optimistic for young unskilled black men. Conventional economic statistics, like wage and employment rates, are based only on the non-institutional population.

For example, the employment-to-population ratio calculated from the monthly Census Bureau household survey, the Current Population Survey, significantly overstates employment rates. Figure 1 shows the employment-to-population ratio for black men without college education, aged 22 to 30. Taking the conventional approach and excluding prison and jail inmates from the population count, employment appears to have declined from 73 to 63 percent, from 1989 to 2004. Once prisoners are counted among the jobless in the population, the percentage employed among young low-education black men falls from 65 to 50 percent. Figure 1 shows that employment rates for young non-college black men did not increase at all through the economic expansion of the late 1990s. The appearance of improved employment in the noninstitutional population was overshadowed by rising incarceration rates.

III. The Labor Market After Prison

While mass incarceration creates a large pool of disadvantaged men who are invisible in conventional labor force statistics, it also diminishes the economic opportunities of those who are released. Researchers have found that men released from incarceration earn less and are employed less than similar men who have not been incarcerated. Estimates of the earnings loss associated with imprisonment range from 10 to 30 percent [4]. A few studies also report that youth detained in correctional facilities before age 20 have higher unemployment and receive lower wages a decade or longer after incarceration [5].

The poor labor market experiences of the formerly incarcerated can be explained in several ways. Those coming out of prison typically have little schooling and erratic work histories. A prison record further deepens this disadvantage.

The stigma of a criminal conviction makes ex-offenders undesirable job applicants in the eyes of employers. Criminal stigma has a legal dimension in which those with criminal records are barred from employment in certain industries and occupations. Incarceration can also deplete skills and foster behaviors that are ill-suited to the open labor market.

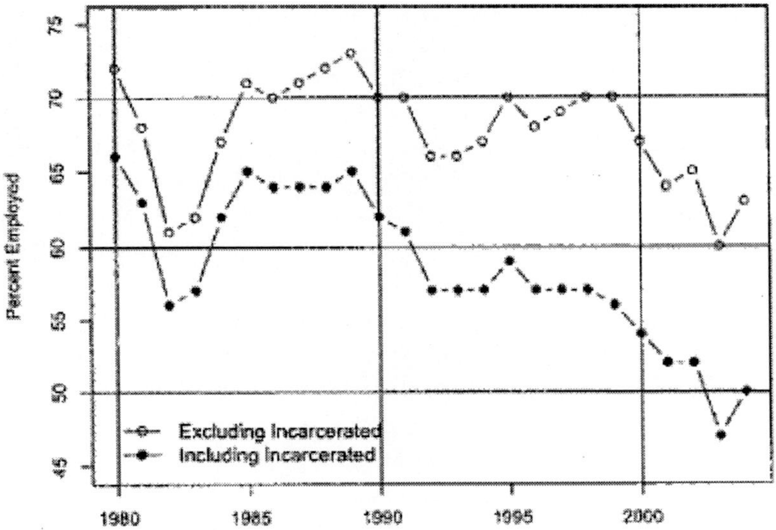

Figure 1. Emplyment-to-population raties for African American men without college education, aged 22 to 30, including and excluding the incarcerated population.

Analysis of the National Longitudinal Survey of Youth (1979) suggests time in prison affects a wide range of employment experiences. The NLSY is a nationally representative survey of youth aged 14 to 20 in 1979. The respondents were interviewed annually until 1994, then every other year after that. From 1979 to 2000, 1 in 5 of the black male respondents were interviewed at least once in a correctional facility.

Statistical analysis shows that imprisonment reduces the hourly wages, annual employment, and annual incomes of young men. Annual employment is reduced by between 10 and 15 percent. Hourly wages are reduced by between 12 and 16 percent. The combined effects of incarceration on hourly wages and annual employment, produce large losses in annual incomes. I find that the annual incomes of formerly incarcerated men are about 35 percent lower than for similar men who have not been incarcerated. We can gain more insight into the kinds of jobs obtained by released prisoners by considering the effects of incarceration on job tenure and wage growth. Analysis of the NLSY shows that the wages of ex-prisoners grow 25 percent more slowly as workers get older. Incarceration is also associated with a one-third reduction in job tenure. These statistics suggest that incarceration channels men into informal, secondary labor market jobs that offer little economic stability or upward mobility.

These effects of incarceration on individual economic status are not new, but they are now playing out on a novel scale. Because returning prisoners are highly concentrated in poor urban neighborhoods, the economic penalties of incarceration now permeate the most economically vulnerable families and communities.

IV. Policy Implications

Because incarceration rates are now so historically high, assistance for re-integration and rehabilitation will be felt not just by those coming out of prison, but by the poor and minority communities from which they originate. Three types of policies would help alleviate the social and economic effects of mass incarceration.

1. Congress should re-examine the large of number of collateral consequences limiting the access of ex-felons to federal benefits and employment. Many restrictions— such as limitations on educational, welfare, and housing benefits—do not serve public safety, impede the reintegration of the formerly incarcerated, and penalize family members.

While restrictions on benefits or employment might be justified if they are closely linked to particular crimes, such restrictions should be strictly time-limited, given the strong pattern of criminal desistance with age.

2. Congress should support prisoner re-entry programs that provide transitional employment and other services. Well-designed programs have been found to improve employment and reduce recidivism. Research suggests that community-based reentry programs should ideally be integrated with education and other programs in prison, and also provide housing, drug treatment, and health care to improve the job readiness of released-prisoners [6]. Post-prison employment would be encouraged by passage of the Second Chance Act of 2007. Employer incentives can be promoted through expansions of the Work Opportunity Tax Credit and the Federal Bonding Program. Taken together, these three measures would provide an important first step to a comprehensive federal re-entry policy.
3. Congress should support the establishment of criminal justice social-impact panels in local jurisdictions that can evaluate unwarranted disparities in juvenile and adult incarceration. By assessing the link between socioeconomic disparities in offending to disparities in incarceration, local social impact panels could identify and take steps to eliminate disproportionate incarceration in poor and minority communities. Social-impact panels could also be charged with assessing disparities that may arise under proposed sentencing reforms.

RESPONSES BY DR. BRUCE WESTERN TO QUESTIONS FROM REPRESENTATIVE ROBERT C. "BOBBY" SCOTT

Question 1. In your testimony, you mentioned creating local social-impact panels. Could you provide more details about these panels, including who would sit on these panels?

Response. Regarding social impact review panels, sentencing commissions at the state and federal levels periodically review demographic patterns in sentencing and other phases of criminal processing. The US Sentencing Commission, for example, is required to collect and publish data on federal sentencing practices. Under its Congressional mandate, the USSC annually publishes figures on the racial, ethnic, age and sex composition of sentenced defendants. The social impact panels I propose would do similar work, drawing on similar expertise and resources as the research arm of the USSC. The panels might ideally be established within state sentencing commissions.

Although the data collection and dissemination tasks would be similar in form to the reporting activities of the USSC, the content would be different. Social impact panels would collect data not just on sentencing but also on arrest, pretrial incarceration, sentenced incarceration, and release. Instead of collecting data just on the race, ethnicity, age, and sex, data would also be obtained on the schooling and residence of those going to prison. This focus on schooling and residence is motivated by the extreme educational and residential disparities in incarceration. Finally, to identify unwarranted disparities, the social impact panels would compare patterns of incarceration to patterns of offending reflected in survey data and data on calls to police. The panel could thus identify localities and social groups whose incarceration rates exceeded their levels of criminal offending. If systematic evidence of disparate incarceration was reported, the panel would work with criminal justice agencies and other stakeholders to eliminate the disparities.

Many of the data resources to conduct this work already exist. Data from the National Corrections Reporting Program provides a demographic census of prison admissions and releases in 38 states. The FBI Uniform Crime Reports and National Incident-Based Reporting System offer detailed counts of offenses known to the police at the county level. The National Crime Victimization Survey of the Bureau of Justice Statistics provides highly detailed demographic information about crime victims. The proposed work of the social impact panels would not build a new statistical system; rather it would extend existing resources with the clear purpose of identifying and mitigating social and residential patterns of disparate incarceration. The social impact panels would also provide advice to policymakers about proposed sentencing and other reforms. By providing this information, policymakers will tend to weigh more heavily the adverse consequences of unwarranted disparities. (A similar and more detailed discussion is provided by Marc Mauer in his proposal for racial impact statements in the 2007 Ohio State Journal of Criminal Law.)

Question 2. In your testimony, you mentioned collateral consequences of incarceration, such as restrictions on participation in public benefit programs. What specific recommendations do you have with regard to these restrictions? What are the negative consequences of having these restrictions?

Response. Regarding collateral consequences of incarceration, individuals with criminal convictions may currently be denied a range of federal benefits. TANF, food stamps, education grants and loans, and federal housing assistance are currently denied to those with felony and misdemeanor records. The 1996 welfare reform established bans on TANF and food stamps for people with felony drug convictions. States could expressly pass exemptions for the denial of benefits and twelve did so while the remainder kept the bans in full or adopted modified restrictions. These bans disproportionately affect poor women with children, a group whose incarceration rate is growing much faster than the general population. I know of no scientific evidence that public safety is served by the denial of TANF and food stamps to individuals with drug convictions. Indeed, rehabilitation and reintegration may well be promoted by such benefits. Many individuals with criminal records have difficulty obtaining work, either because they lack job skills or because employers have policies against hiring individuals with prior convictions. Public assistance and food stamps provide such individuals with necessary survival assistance as they look for employment. Public assistance and food stamps also help ensure the continued availability of alcohol and drug treatment programs. Alcohol and drug treatment programs, particularly residential programs, have historically relied on funding from a client's public assistance and food stamps to pay for room and board. Without these funds, programs are forced to reduce services. Because they might adversely affect public safety. Congress should eliminate bans on TANF and food stamps for those with drug convictions.

In 1998 the Higher Education Act was amended to disqualify those with felony and misdemeanor drug convictions from eligibility for post-secondary aid from Pell Grants, Stafford loans, and work-study assistance. Lifetime ineligibility is imposed on those with three convictions for drug possession or two convictions for drug sales. The GAO estimates that from 2001 to 2003, around 140,000 applicants for federal education assistance were denied because of a drug conviction. The number affected is likely to be much larger, because the ban on those with drug conviction discourages many from applying. Low education is perhaps the dominant deficit, besides the criminal record itself, limiting the economic opportunities of those released from incarceration. As for the ban on TANF and food stamps, I know of no scientific evidence that the ban on post-secondary education assistance promotes public safety. Indeed, the ban on post-secondary education for those with drug convictions is more likely to lead to recidivism than desistance from crime. Because higher education supports are targeted at low-income students, banning post-secondary aid compounds the economic difficulties that those with criminal records are struggling to overcome. Congress should eliminate the denial of federal post secondary education benefits to individuals with drug convictions.

Finally, a variety of provisions deny federally assisted housing benefits to those involved in drug-related activity. Federal law provides for two main exclusions. Those engaging in drug-related activity in public housing can be evicted, and applications for public housing can be denied to those with convictions for drug-related activities.

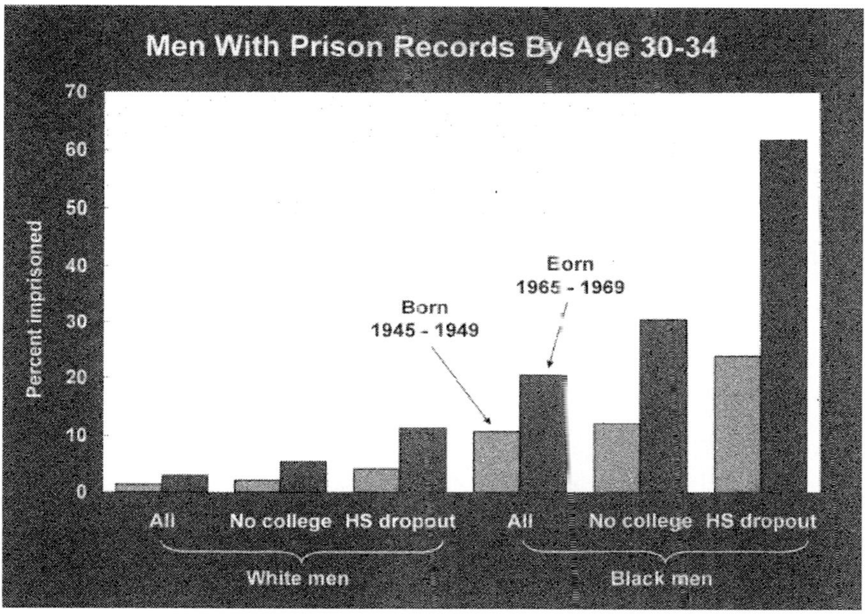

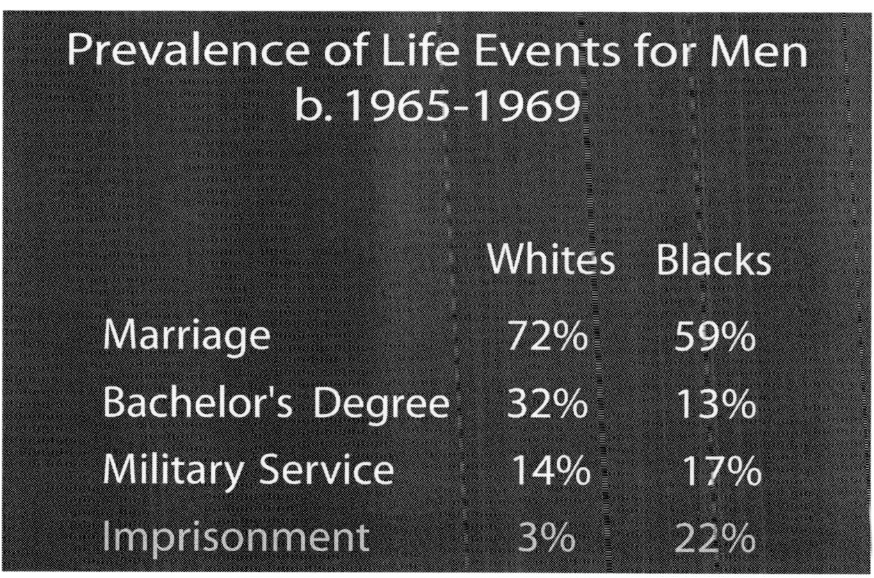
Prevalence of Life Events for Men b. 1965-1969

	Whites	Blacks
Marriage	72%	59%
Bachelor's Degree	32%	13%
Military Service	14%	17%
Imprisonment	3%	22%

Pay and Employment Among Ex-Prisoners (NLSY)

	Incarceration Effect
Hourly Wages	26%
Annual Weeks Worked	-6.9 weeks
Log Annual Earnings	42%
Rate of Hourly Wage Growth	27%
Job Tenure	34%

Drug-related serious violence is an acute problem in public housing. However, there is little evidence that the denial of housing to those with drug convictions has reduced crime public housing. Public housing, like education and welfare benefits, helps erase a key deficit for those returning home from prison and jail. In the absence of evidence that the denial of public housing to those with drug convictions improves public safety, and in light of the vast number of poor citizens with drug convictions, Congress should eliminate ineligibility for public housing on the basis of a criminal record.

PREPARED STATEMENT OF ALPHONSO ALBERT, EXECUTIVE DIRECTOR, SECOND CHANCES

The Second Chances program is a program sponsored by the city of Norfolk to assist non-violent offenders that are returning back into the local community after being incarcerated in jail and prison.

Over the past eight years, Second Chances has served more than 1200 offenders, provided more than 900 jobs at an average wage of $9.00 per hour and maintained a 73 percent employment retention rate over one year period. Additionally, Second Chances has implemented programs to serve children of incarcerated parents, opened a permanent supportive housing initiative to provide housing for offenders that are homeless upon their return and started three business enterprises that hire program participants at a minimum of $ 8 per hour and $12 per hour with benefits when they have drivers license.

There is a collateral cost to incarceration however, that is rarely observed or talked about but one that comes back to haunt society in so many other ways. The cost is one that impacts families and children of incarcerated individuals. Most incarcerated individuals have families and many of them have children that grow-up themselves to be incarcerated. The fact that a child that lives in a household with a loved one or family member that has been incarcerated and will likely be incarcerated themselves when they grow up is due in large measure to the fact that the same conditions that existed for the adult will exist for the child unless there is some intervening factors. Limited education, lack of positive role model, poor housing conditions, abuse, etc. are all factors that contribute. The Second Chances staff recently conducted a survey of women in the Norfolk City jail that were within 90 days of release. The results of the survey indicated that and that 34 women had children between the ages of 4–18, only 9 of the 34 had legal custody of their children, 25 or the 34 self reported as having problems with substance abuse or addiction, 16 admitted having damaged relationship with family as a result of their addiction, and 27 acknowledged that they needed some type of parenting class or training in order to be a better parents.

The greatest challenge that we face on a daily basis in helping offenders make a positive transition from prison back into the community (getting out and staying out as productive citizens) is pre-release planning and post release services. The department of corrections provides limited training opportunities for returning offenders and has only recently began focusing re-entry planning as a part of their overall strategy for helping offenders make a smooth transition back into local communities. More often than not, the issues of no proper identification, no birth certificates, limited pre-release plans, no post release services, housing and lack of job leads, financial burden and hardship are all things that stifle the offenders and prevent the individual from having a positive re-entry experience. These factors also lead to recidivism and relapse in so many of the cases that we see on a daily basis.

Recently, the State of Virginia became one of seven states around the country to participate in the National Governors Association Reentry Policy Academy. Virginia sub sequentially established five pilot programs around the State that focused on providing pre-release planning and post release services. The challenge to these pilot sites however, is lack of funding. Lack of funding means no counselors to work with offenders prior to release in getting proper Identification, birth certificates and a total of all fines, court cost, child support, restitution and other financial obligations prior to release. Funding at the federal level would also support staffing that helps offenders with job leads, housing placement, job training and other post release services. It is my opinion that funding for reentry programs that provide pre and post release planning as well as job placement, case management and follow- up aftercare should be made available in order to help prevent recidivism, strengthen families, and promote healthy communities through the concept of investing in our human infrastructure at a time when we can least afford not to do so.

Thank you for the opportunity to provide testimony to this committee and I would be pleased to answer any further questions.

RESPONSES BY ALPHONSO ALBERT TO QUESTIONS FROM REPRESENTATIVE ROBERT C. "BOBBY" SCOTT

Question 1. In your testimony, you mention the importance of pre-release planning and post-release services. How would you recommend integrating these ideas into the current criminal justice and incarceration system and what effect would the re-institution of parole have on an inmate's incentive to plan for release.

Response. Pre-release planning and post release services could be integrated into the current system by funding directed to the state re-entry pilots and programs that are currently providing pre and post release services as beginning models. Funding that would provide each pilot site with two pre-release counselors per facility that would be responsible for assisting offenders with securing id cards, birth certificates, clothing, an assessment of all fines and financial obligations prior to release as well as two or three weeks of orientation that prepares the offenders for what to expect when returning. Funding for the same pilot for post release services would help with transitional jobs, case managers, housing vouchers, transportation assistance, life skills, job training and other related services.

As far as the parole board, I do think that having parole adds incentive to an inmates when incarcerated and motivates positive behavior and outlook for inmate. I also feel however that the compromise achieved when selecting a parole board in the past (and by compromise, I mean the people selected) has been too political and influenced too heavily by people that either advocate revenge or victim rights. This does not allow for an objective viewing of the risk factors and suitability of inmate parole candidates. I am strongly in favor of reinstituting the parole system here in Virginia, however; the board should be selected differently.

I certainly hope that I have answered your questions satisfactorily and please feel free to contact me if I can be of further assistance.

Prepared Statement of Michael Jacobson, Director, Vera Institute of Justice

Good morning Senator Webb. I would like to thank you for inviting me here to testify today. I have some brief remarks and then I'd be happy to answer any questions you might have.

The United States now spends over $60 billion annually to maintain its corrections system reflecting the fact that we imprison a greater percentage of our population than any other nation on earth. In the last 30 years, we have seen the jail and prison population rise from 250 thousand to almost 2.3 million, almost a tenfold increase.

The strain that this geometric increase in those incarcerated puts on our states and cities is cumulative and continues to grow. Over the last decade and a half, the only function of state governments to grow as a percentage of overall state budgets is, with the exception of Medicaid, corrections. The rate of growth of spending on corrections in state budgets exceeds that for education, health care, social services, transportation and environmental protection. There is a very clear relationship between the amount of money we spend on prisons and the amount that is available, or not available, for all these other essential areas of government. In many states—California is one that especially comes to mind—one can literally see money move in the budget from primary and secondary education to prisons. State budgets tend to be largely zero sum games and increases in corrections spending has absolutely held down spending in these other areas of government, many of which are also directly related to public safety.

Of course, the obvious question this raises is, "what do we get for that money?"Certainly, there should be some significant connection between our tremendous use of prison and public safety. As most people know, the U.S. experienced a large crime decline from the early 1990s to the early 2000s and it would seem to make intuitive sense that our significantly increasing prison systems played a major role in that decline.

In fact, it is a much more mixed and nuanced story than it would appear. There is some consensus among criminologists and social scientists that over the last decade, our increased use of prison was responsible for some (perhaps around 20–25 percent) but by no means most of the national crime decline. Additionally, there is also agreement that, going forward, putting even more people in prison will have declining effectiveness as we put more and more people in prison who present less and less of a threat to public safety. At this point, putting greater numbers of people into prison as a way to achieve more public safety is one of the least effective ways we know to decrease crime.

We know, for instance, that even after spending tens of billions of dollars on incarceration, more than half of those leaving prison are back in prison within three years—not a result that anybody should be proud of. We know that targeted spending for effective in-prison and post-prison reentry programs will reduce crime and victims more substantially than prison expansion. We know that diverting people from prison who are not threats to public safety into serious and structured community based alternatives to prison is more effective than simply continuing to incarcerate, at huge expense, these same people. In the same vein, the research shows that increasing high school graduation rates, neighborhood based law enforcement initiatives and increases in employment and wages will also more effectively reduce crime than greater use of prison.

We also know that incarcerating so much of our population and especially the disproportionate incarceration of people of color also comes with other costs as well. Hundreds of thousands of people leave prison annually with no right to vote, no access to public housing, hugely limited abilities to find employment and high levels of drug use and mental illness. These unintended consequences of incarceration ripple through families and communities as those returning home are overwhelmed by seemingly intractable obstacles. Not surprisingly, many people wind up returning to prison in astounding numbers, further draining scarce resources that could be made available to deal with some of these obstacles themselves.

As someone who used to run the largest city jail system in the country, I know that most people who leave jail and prison do not want to come back. It is a miserable and degrading experience and my colleagues who run these systems and I always marvel about the numbers of people who are leaving prison who want to make good and do good. Once they leave however, they are confronted by such overwhelming barriers on which we currently spend almost no money or attention that no one should be surprised that these same people are back in prison so soon.

We know that states can continue to decrease crime and simultaneously decrease prison populations. New York State, for example, has for the last seven years seen the largest decrease in its prison population of any state in the nation—a decline of 14 percent. The rest of the states increased their prison populations by an average of 12 percent over the same time period. At the same time, violent crime decreased in New York State by 20 percent compared to just over 1 percent for the rest of the country. Prison populations can drop along with crime and victimization.

If we were serious about using our limited resources most effectively in reducing crime and victimization and increasing public safety, then we would begin to responsibly and systematically transfer some of the resources now used to imprison people to community based prevention, reentry and capacity building. It is important to stress here that this is an issue of public safety. Even putting aside all arguments about efficiency and effectiveness, talking only in terms of public safety, we will all be safer if we begin to reinvest some of the money that now goes to incarcerate people who do not pose a threat to public safety (and who become more of a threat to public safety after they are imprisoned) into other programmatic initiatives both inside and outside the criminal justice system.

The fact is that almost all the extant research points out that our prison system is too big, too expensive, drains funds away from other essential areas that can more effectively increase public safety, and is harmful to our poorest communities. Despite all this research, however, we continue to imprison more and more people. There are a host of reasons for this ongoing trend including: the attraction of prisons as engines of economic development for rural communities; the financial incentives for public employee unions as well as for the private prison industry in more spending on prisons; the "realities" of the budget process and constrained budgets that limit opportunities to make substantial investments in new initiatives; and the omnipresent hyper-politics that surround issues of crime and punishment in the United States.

These are all formidable obstacles but none should be sufficient to keep us from educating policymakers and the public that there is a better way to be safe and have less crime.

Responses by Dr. Michael P. Jacobson to Questions from Representative Robert C. "Bobby" Scott

Question 1. In your testimony, you reference the need to invest in capacity building. Could you elaborate on what capacity building means in this context?

Response. The context in which I was using "capacity building" was around improving the civic infrastructure in high incarceration communities. For instance, if you superimposed on the map of New York City that Dr. Loury brought showing high impact communities in New York City, you would also find that these same communities generally have the lowest performing schools, the fewest health and child care facilities, the fewest financial institutions, community centers, after- school programs etc. It is no coincidence that the communities that "contribute" the greatest numbers of state prisoners are also so lacking in adequate civic infrastructure. In addition to directing funding away from prisons and to alternatives to prisons, community based reentry programming and treatment, it is important to consider the essential needs and services of these communities as well.

Question 2. Please describe the essential elements of successful crime reduction programs.

Response. In terms of the essential elements of crime reduction programs, any successful crime reduction strategy must consist of more than simply increased criminal justice resources. We know, for instance, that targeted investments in education programs (especially those that increase high school graduation rates), employment programs and wages, and treatment all have the potential to decrease crime by a greater amount than just simply more use of prison (where we know the impact will be minimal) and generally increasing the number of police (though particular policing strategies can be very effective). The overall point here is that if we are serious about reducing crime the research tells us we have to look at investments outside the criminal justice system in addition to whatever we fund in criminal justice. The politics may not work as well, but the research tells us that specific funding in education, employment, wages, and treatment can have a significant impact on reducing crime. (See Stemen, Don. Reconsidering Incarceration: New Directions for Reducing Crime, Vera Institute of Justice, January 2007.)

PREPARED STATEMENT OF PAT NOLAN, VICE PRESIDENT, PRISON FELLOWSHIP

Mr. Chairman and members, I am grateful for this opportunity to share with you some thoughts on the cost to our society of the massive increase in incarceration in the United States. Thank you for holding this hearing to address this very important topic. Others have discussed the financial cost of mass imprisonment. I will try to give you some perspective on the human toll it is taking.

My name is Pat Nolan. I am a Vice President of Prison Fellowship and lead their criminal justice reform arm, Justice Fellowship. I also serve on the Prison

Rape Elimination Commission and the Commission on Safety and Abuse in America's Prisons. I bring a unique background to this work. I served for 15 years as a member of the California State Assembly, four of those as the Assembly Republican Leader. I was a leader on crime issues, particularly on behalf of victims' rights. I was one of the original sponsors of the Victims' Bill of Rights (Proposition 15) and was awarded the "Victims Advocate Award" by Parents of Murdered Children. I was prosecuted for a campaign contribution I accepted, which turned out to be part of an FBI sting. I pleaded guilty to one count of racketeering, and served 29 months in federal custody.

Now, God has placed me in a position that I can share these observations with criminal justice officials, using my experiences as a lawyer, legislator and prisoner to improve our justice system. Justice Fellowship works with government officials at the federal and state levels, helping them develop policies that repair the harm done to victims, reform the hearts of offenders, and, in doing that, restore peace to communities.

The figures on incarceration are staggering. One in every 32 adult Americans is in prison or on supervised release. Prisons have become one of the fastest growing items in state budgets, siphoning off dollars that that might otherwise be available for schools, roads or hospitals.

In America today, offenders serve their sentences in overcrowded prisons where they are exposed to the horrors of violence including rape, isolation from family and friends, and despair. The best way to I can describe how it felt to be imprisoned is that I was like an amputee. I was cutoff from my family, my friends, my work, my church and my community. Then, with my stumps still bleeding, I was tossed into a roiling cauldron of anger, bitterness, despair and often violence.

Most inmates are idle in prison, warehoused with little preparation to make better choices when they return to the free world. Just one-third of all released prisoners will have received vocational or educational training in prison. While approximately three of every four inmates have a substance abuse problem, less than 20 percent will have had any substance abuse treatment before they are released. The number of returning inmates is now four times what it was 20 years ago, yet there are fewer programs to prepare them return to their communities. They get little preparation to make better choices when they return to the free world. On leaving prison they will have great difficulty finding employment. The odds are great that their first incarceration will not be their last.

Our large investment in our prisons might be justified if the inmates released from them were reformed in hearts as well as habits. However, most inmates do not leave prison transformed into law-abiding citizens. In fact, the very skills inmates develop to survive inside prison make them anti-social when they are released.

More than 700,000 inmates will be released from America's prisons next year. To put this in perspective, that is more than three times the size of the United States Marine Corps. Even more will be released the following year, and even more every year thereafter. Each day, over 1,900 offenders leave prison and return to neighborhoods across the country.

What has been done to prepare these returning inmates to live healthy, productive, law-abiding lives? What kind of neighbors will they be? Each of us has a stake in seeing that these men and women make a safe and successful return to their communities. Yet, very little is being done to help them make that transition successfully.

The fact of the matter is most of the inmates we have released do commit more crimes. Over the last 30 years, the rate of rearrest has hovered stubbornly around 67 percent. If two-thirds of the patients leaving a hospital had to be readmitted, we would quickly find a new hospital. So also, we must find a better way to prepare inmates for their release if we are to have safer communities. One way is through the Second Chance Act which is now before the Senate. It will provide the states and our communities help in developing better ways to do that.

However, we must also examine sentencing laws that put so many non-violent offenders in prison. Certainly we need prisons to separate violent and dangerous people from the rest of society. But given the overcrowding and violence in our prisons, why on earth would we put people convicted of non-violent crimes in prison? Prisons are for people we are afraid of, but our sentencing laws have filled them with people we are merely angry at. Changing our sentences so that low risk offenders are punished in the community under strict supervision would reduce overcrowding in prisons and help control violence. It would hold low risk offenders accountable without exposing them to the violence and the great difficulties of transition back to the community after their sentence.

After release from prison, offenders face many barriers, often called "invisible punishments": They are frequently denied parental rights, driver's licenses, student loans, the right to vote, and residency in public housing—which is often the only housing that they can afford.

Further, little is done to change the moral perspective of offenders. Most inmates do not leave prison transformed into law-abiding citizens; in fact, the very skills inmates develop to survive inside prison make them anti social when they are released. Most are given a bus ticket to their hometown, gate money of between $10 and $200, and infrequently a new set of clothes. Upon leaving prison virtually all will have great difficulty finding employment.

The moment offenders step off the bus they face several critical decisions: Where will they live, where will they be able to find a meal, where should they look for a job, how will they get to a job interview, and where can they earn enough money to pay for necessities? These returning inmates are also confronted with many details of personal business, such as obtaining identification cards and documents, making medical appointments, and working through the many everyday bureaucratic problems that occur during any transition. These choices prompt feelings of intense stress and worry over the logistics of their return to the outside world. To someone who has had no control over any aspect of their lives for many years, each of these problems can be difficult. In accumulation, they can be overwhelming.

My own experience provides a good example. Shortly after my release from prison to the halfway house, some friends took me to lunch at a local deli. The waiter came over to take our orders. Everyone else told him what they wanted, but I kept poring over the menu. My eyes raced over the columns of choices. I knew that I was supposed to order, but the number of options overwhelmed me. My friends sat in embarrassed silence. I was paralyzed. The waiter looked at me impatiently. I began to panic. How ridiculous that I wasn't able to do such a simple thing as order lunch. Finally, in desperation I ordered the next item my eyes landed on, a turkey sandwich. I didn't even want it, but at least it put an end to this embarrassing incident.

For two years I hadn't been allowed to make any choices about what I ate. Now I was having a hard time making a simple choice that most people face every day. If I had this much difficulty after only a couple of years in prison, think how hard it is for those inmates who haven't made any choices for 5, 10, or 15 years. And what about those who didn't have the wonderful home, the loving family, the strong faith and the good education that I had? They face a baffling array of options and little preparation. Is it any surprise that so many newly released prisoners make some bad choices and end up back in prison?

The choices offenders make immediately after release are extremely important. Of the ex-prisoners who fail, over half will be arrested within the first 6 months. That is not much time to turn their lives around. One study of rearrests in New York City found that the rate was especially high during the first hours and days following release. This early window of time is the most intense period for ex-prisoners, when they may be overwhelmed by the accumulation of large and small decisions facing them. On average, ex-offenders have only a one-in-three chance of getting through their first three years without being arrested.

As the number of people released from prison and jail increases steadily, we cannot afford to continue to send them home with little preparation. These policies have harmed too many victims, destroyed too many families, overwhelmed too many communities, and wasted too many lives as they repeat the cycle of arrest, incarceration, release and rearrest. The toll this system takes is not measured merely in human lives: The strain on taxpayers has been tremendous. As jail and prison populations have soared, so have corrections budgets, creating fiscal crises in virtually every state and squeezing money for schools, health care, and roads from state budgets.

It does not have to be this way. Fortunately, there are many things that the government in partnership with the community, and in particular our churches, can do that increase the likelihood that inmates will return safely to our communities.

One of the most important provisions of the Second Chance Act will provide grants to community and faith-based non-profits to link offenders and their families with mentors. Let me tell you why this is so important.

It is essential that returning inmates have a friend they can turn to as they take their difficult first steps in freedom. A loving mentor can help them think through their decisions and hold them accountable for making the right moral choices.

The importance of mentors to returning prisoners was stressed by Dr. Byron Johnson in his recent study of the Texas InnerChange Freedom Initiative (IFI), the reentry program operated by Prison Fellowship under contract with the state. Dr. Johnson's study found that IFI graduates were two and a half times less likely to be reincarcerated than inmates in a matched comparison group. The two-year post-release reincarceration rate among IFI graduates in Texas was 8 percent, compared with 20.3 percent of the matched group.

Dr. Johnson emphasized that mentors were ''absolutely critical'' to the impressive results. The support and accountability provided by mentors often make the difference between a successful return to society and re-offending. As these offenders make the difficult transition back into the community, they need relationships with caring, moral adults. The greater the density of good people we pack around them, the greater the chance that they will be successfully replanted into the community.

IFI recruits members of local churches to give at least 1 hour a week to mentor the IFI inmates, both while they are still incarcerated and after they return to their community. In his interviews with the IFI participants, Dr. Johnson found that the mentors' weekly visits were very important to the inmates. ''Without exception, IFI participants have indicated the critical impact volunteers have made in their lives. The sincerity and time commitment of volunteers has simply overwhelmed program participants." The benefit of these relationships with their mentors derives not only from the things discussed, but also for the love conveyed. By faithfully keeping their commitment to the weekly mentoring sessions, the mentors show a commitment to the inmates that many have never experienced before in their lives. As Dr. Martin Luther King, Jr., said, ''To change someone, you must first love them, and they must know that you love them."While many people would never associate the word ''love" with prisoners, love is precisely what has been lacking in the lives of many of these men and women. They have gone through life without anyone caring about them or what they do, nor caring enough about them to coach them as they confront life. Many inmates are emotionally overdrawn checkbooks. We must make deposit, after deposit, after deposit before we will see any positive balance.

A mentor can help the ex-offenders think through employment options and tell them what their employer will expect of them on the job. Many offenders have never had someone in their lives who has held a steady job. They have no model for being a good employee. A mentor can teach them that they need to get up on time, go to work each day, and call their supervisor if they must be late or absent. Offenders may find it difficult to take direction or may lack skills to cope with a difficult boss or fellow employees. A mentor can help them with these and other everyday difficulties of the workplace and teach them the importance of punctuality, politeness, and diplomacy on the job.

Mentors help returning inmates deal with many of the personal problems they typically encounter upon leaving prison: no reliable friends outside their former gang network, marital problems, and no easy way to get on with life.

Mentors can also help the offenders learn decisionmaking skills and teach them how to keep track of bills and pay them on time. In prison, inmates do not have to deal with any of this. On the street such details may quickly overwhelm them.

In short, offenders need to be taught how to make good choices, handle responsibility, and be accountable—to make the right choice even when no one is looking.

Corrections staff can't make this kind of commitment to help each individual prisoner. But volunteer mentors can, and, in fact are, making this commitment in programs throughout the country.

Most of us can remember a teacher, coach, or neighbor who believed in us and helped us believe in ourselves. That is exactly what returning offenders need, yet most have never had someone like that in their lives. Mentors can fill that void. A loving mentor lets returning inmates know that the community is invested in their success. And the Second Chance Act will provide concrete assistance to community and faith-based groups to recruit and train mentors for this essential work.

As you work to improve our criminal justice programs, I suggest you keep several concepts in mind:

The purpose of our criminal justice system is to create safer communities and reduce the number of victims. There is a tendency to focus on institutional safety, rather than community safety. Under this narrow, institutional focus, the surest way to avoid escapes and riots would be to keep prisoners in their cells 24 hours a day, 7 days a week However, the public would be in far greater danger after those prisoners were released. Instead of focusing on institutional convenience, correctional policy must be judged by whether it makes the public safer.

Reentry planning should start at intake. Planning for the release of inmates should start as soon as they are sentenced. Assignment to a prison should include factors such as the proximity of the prison to the inmate's family and the availability of needed programs.

Prison policies should strengthen families. Crime not only has a devastating impact on the direct victims, but also on the families of offenders. Incarceration puts tremendous stress on the spouses and children of offenders. These family members have committed no crime. The stress on the family is exacerbated by policies such as placing inmates far from their families, frequently treating visiting families with disrespect, and charging exorbitant fees for telephone calls.

In addition, there are often preexisting issues of drug abuse, physical abuse, and marital conflict. If these issues are not resolved during incarceration, reentry will be much more difficult. Programs such as La Bodega de la Familia in New York, work with the entire family to strengthen their relationships. A healthy, functioning family is one of the most important predictors for successful reentry. Our prison policies must be changed to strengthen families rather than destabilize them.

Prisons are for people we're afraid of, but many of those filling our prisons are there because we are merely mad at them. The response to a technical violation should not automatically result in return to prison. Obviously, it is important for offenders to learn to live by the rules. However, if an offender is making good progress it makes little sense to throw that all away because he didn't file his paperwork on time or missed a meeting with his probation officer. One judge told me, "Right now, I can either send him back to prison or let him go to the beach. Give me something in between."Inmates should be encouraged to participate in faith based programs. To deal effectively with crime, we must first understand it. At its root, crime is a moral problem. Offenders make bad moral choices that result in harm to their victims. To break the cycle of crime, we must address this immoral behavior. There aren't enough police officers to stop everyone tempted to do something bad from doing it; inmates must rely on inner restraint to keep from harming others.

Job training and education alone won't transform an inmate from a criminal into a law-abiding citizen. For some inmates such programs merely make them smarter, more sophisticated criminals. It is a changed heart that can transform a prisoner. Unfortunately, many prison programs ignore the moral aspect of crime and avoid all discussion of faith and morality. In doing so, they are missing a significant factor that has proven very effective at changing criminals' behavior faith. If inmates are to live healthy, productive, law-abiding lives when they return to their communities, we must equip them with moral standards to live up to and a world view that explains why they should do so.

The community should "own" reentry. There is a tendency to view reentry as a program of corrections departments. While our prison systems are certainly central to the reentry process, it is the community that has the most at stake. Many corrections policies make it difficult for community and church groups to be involved in preparing inmates for release. Many systems "keep their options open" on release dates, often right up to the day of release, making it impossible to recruit, match and train mentors, locate appropriate housing, arrange for jobs or welcome the inmates at the bus. For reentry programs to be a success, community groups and churches should be viewed as important partners with the state, not as mere auxiliaries.

An important example of a corrections policy that makes reentry much more difficult is the so-called "non-fraternization" rule. I am sure you will be shocked to learn that the Federal Bureau of Prisons and many states DOCs prohibit religious volunteers from being in contact with inmates after they are released. This policy cuts the inmates off from the very people most likely to be able to help them make a successful transition. Corrections policies must be rewritten to encourage mentoring relationships to begin inside prison and continue after release. These healthy relationships should be encouraged, not prohibited. I am told the BOP is considering changes to this policy, but to make sure the Second Chance Act will overturn this counterproductive policy.

Programs are important, but healthy relationships are even more important. The support and accountability provided by mentors often make the difference between a successful return to society and re-offending. As offenders make the difficult transition back into the community, they need relationships with caring, moral adults. The greater the density of good people we pack around them, the greater the chance that they will be successfully replanted back into the community.

I have written a book, When Prisoners Return, which covers all these issues and is being used by departments of corrections, churches and community organizations to coordinate their efforts to help offenders during the difficult transition from prison to the community. If you and your staff would like copies, I will gladly provide them to you.

I mentioned that I serve on the Commission on Safety and Abuse in America's Prisons. Last year we released our report "Confronting Confinement". It concluded that our prisons are breeding grounds for future crime. The overcrowding and lack of educational and rehabilitative programming are spawning violence behind bars that spills over into our neighborhoods once prisoners are released.

The Commission made several recommendations based on a clear consensus among the experts that to prevent violence in prison we must:

- Reduce crowding.
- Increase access to meaningful programs and activities.
- Encourage a climate of mutual respect between staff and inmates.
- Increase the transparency of the institutions by increasing accessibility to outside agencies and volunteers.
- Identify at-risk prisoners and potential predators, and classify them accordingly.
- Make better use of surveillance technology.
- Strengthen family relationships by placing inmates close to their families, encouraging family visits, and lowering the cost of phone calls.

At Prison Fellowship, an outreach founded by Chuck Colson, we have had 31 years of experience in seeking the transformation of prisoners' lives. We have identified six "best practices" that we believe are applicable in almost any prison setting to achieve transformation in the lives of prisoners resulting in lower recidivism and greater public safety.

a. Community—men or women living together on a floor, wing, or building with the intentional purpose of transforming their lives.
b. Consistency—being able to work with prisoners on a frequent and consistent basis—daily if possible
c. Character—a focus on the moral and personal issues that led to criminal behavior

d. Comprehensive—holistic in nature and includes spiritual formation, education, vocational training, substance abuse treatment, life skills training, parenting training, etc.
e. Continuous—it begins in prison and continues in as they are released from prison into the community.
f. Collaborative—it is a collaborative process that must involve many individuals, government agencies, the business community, faith based institutions, and nonprofits.

As a state legislator I made the mistake of thinking that locking people up made our communities safer. Only when I was in prison did I realize that most inmates will be released someday, and locking so many of our people in prison while doing nothing to prepare them for their release is very dangerous. I commend this committee and your staff for calling attention to the horrible toll that overincarceration is taking on American society.

PREPARED STATEMENT OF CONGRESSWOMAN SHEILA JACKSON-LEE, OF TEXAS

Thank you, Chairman Schumer and Vice-Chairwoman Maloney for holding this important and timely hearing on the exponential growth of the prison population in the United States. Thank you also for allowing me to share with the Joint Economic Committee a legislative proposal I have been advocating for several years which help alleviate this crisis.

As members of this Committee are fully aware, the United States has experienced a sharp increase in its prison population in the past 30 years. From the 1920s to the mid-1970s, the incarceration rate in the United States remained steady at approximately 110 prisoners per 100,000 people. Today, the incarceration rate is 737 inmates per 100,000 residents, comprising 2.1 million persons in federal, state, and local prisons. The United States has 5 percent of the world's population but now has 25 percent of its prisoners. There are approximately 5 million Americans under the supervision of the correctional system, including parole, probation, and other community supervision sanctions.

When it comes to the plight of African American and Hispanic males, the numbers paint an even bleaker picture. Incarceration is not an equal opportunity punishment. For example, incarceration rates in the United States by race were:

- Blacks: 2,468 per 100,000
- Latinos: 1,038 per 100,000
- Whites: 409 per 100,000

Gender is an important "filter" on who goes to prison or jail, June 30, 2006. Males are 10 times as likely to end in prison as females:

- Females: 134 per 100,000
- Males: 1,384 per 100,000

Looking at just the males by race, the incarceration rates become even more frightening, June 30, 2006:

- Black males: 4,789 per 100,000
- Latino males: 1,862 per 100,000
- White males: 736 per 100,000

Looking at males aged 25–29 and by race, you can see what is going on even clearer, June 30, 2006:

- For White males ages 25–29: 1,685 per 100,000.
- For Latino males ages 25–29: 3,912 per 100,000.
- For Black males ages 25–29: 11,695 per 100,000. (That's 11.7 percent of Black men in their late 20s.)

Here is another statistic that I find particularly striking. The United States locks up its Black males at a rate 5.8 times higher than the most openly racist country in the world ever did:

- South Africa under apartheid (1993), Black males: 851 per 100,000
- United States (2006), Black males: 4,789 per 100,000

In Texas, the state from which both President Bush and I hail, the situation is just as bad. Texas has an African American population of 11 percent but an African American prison population of 44 percent. Texas also ranks number first in putting citizens to death. It ranks third in spending on prisons but 20th in education spending. It ranks 15th in incarcerating drug offenders.

Mr. Chairman, this state of affairs is not sustainable. The costs of maintaining this "prison-industrial complex" annually consume an increasing share of public revenues and adversely impacts society's ability to make other needed public investments in education, health care, infrastructure, and economic growth. That is why I am pleased that the Joint Economic Committee is holding this hearing today to examine why the United States has such a disproportionate share of the world's prison population, as well as ways to address this issue that responsibly balance public safety and the high social and economic costs of imprisonment.

According to the Urban Institute, "the social and economic costs to the nation are enormous." With 2.25 million people incarcerated in approximately five thousand prisons and jails, the combined expenditures of local governments, state governments, and the federal government for law enforcement and corrections personnel totals over $200 billion.

I have reintroduced legislation in this Congress which addresses an important cause of the prison population explosion, and that is the continued warehousing of elderly and middle-aged non-violent offenders. My legislation, H.R. 261, the "Federal Prison Bureau Nonviolent Offender Relief Act," provides for the early release for non-violent offenders who have attained the age of at least 45 years of age, have never been convicted of a violent crime, have never escaped or attempted to escape from incarceration, and have not engaged in any violation, involving violent conduct, of institutional disciplinary regulations.

My bill seeks to ensure that in affording offenders a second chance to turn around their lives and contribute to society, ex-offenders are not too old to take advantage of a second chance to redeem themselves. A secondary benefit of my legislation is that it would relieve the some of the strain on federal, state, and local government budgets by reducing considerably government expenditures on warehousing prisoners.

Mr. Chairman, some of those who are incarcerated face extremely long sentences, and this language would help to address this problem. Releasing rehabilitated, middle-aged, non-violent offenders from an already overcrowded prison population can be a win-win situation for society and the individual who, like the Jean Valjean made famous in Victor Hugo's Les Miserables, is redeemed by the grace of a second chance. The reentry of such individuals into the society will enable them to repay the community through community service and obtain or regain a sense of self- worth and accomplishment. It promises a reduction in burdens to the taxpayer, and an affirmation of the America value that no non-violent offender is beyond redemption.

Mr. Chairman, at a time when tight budgets have forced many states to consider the early release of hundreds of inmates to conserve tax revenue and when our nation's Social Security system is in danger of being totally privatized, early release is a common-sense option to raise capital.

The rate of incarceration and the length of sentence for first-time, non-violent offenders have become extreme. Over the past two decades, no area of state government expenditures has increased as rapidly as prisons and jails. According to data collected by the Justice Department, the number of prisoners in America has more than tripled over the last two decades from 500,000 to 1.8 million, with states like California and Texas experiencing eightfold prison population increases during that time. Mr. Chairman, there are more people in the prisons of America than there are residents in states of Alaska, North Dakota, and Wyoming combined.

Over one million people have been warehoused for nonviolent, often petty crimes. The European Union, with a population of 370 million, has one-sixth the number of incarcerated persons as we do, and that includes violent and nonviolent offenders. This is one third the number of prisoners which America, a country with 70 million fewer people, incarcerates for nonviolent offenses.

The 1.1 million nonviolent offenders we currently lock up represents five times the number of people held in India's entire prison system, even though its population is four times greater than the United States.

As the number of individuals incarcerated for nonviolent offenses has steadily risen, African-Americans and Latinos have comprised a growing percentage of the overall number incarcerated. In the 1930s, 75 percent of the people entering state and federal prison were white (roughly reflecting the demographics of the nation). Today, minority communities represent 70 percent of all new admissions—and more than half of all Americans behind bars.

As I have stated, my legislation will ensure that in affording offenders a second chance to turn around their lives and contribute to society, ex-offenders are not too old to take advantage of a second chance to redeem themselves. My legislation will also relieve the some of the strain on federal, state, and local government budgets by reducing considerably government expenditures on warehousing prisoners.

For these reasons, I commend to your attention H.R. 261, the "Federal Prison Bureau Nonviolent Offender Relief Act," and ask you to give this proposal due consideration.

Chairman Schumer, Vice-Chairwoman Maloney, let me express again my appreciation to you and the members of the Joint Economic Committee for holding this hearing and allowing me to submit this statement.

Thank you.

NOTES

[1] Pastore and Maguire (2007).
[2] Western (2006, 29).
[3] Western (2006, 16).
[4] Grogger (1995), Lott (1990), Waldfogel (1994), Western (2002).
[5] Freeman (1992) and Western and Beckett (1999).
[6] Positive effects of employment and education programs in prison and after are reported by Saylor and Gaes (1997, 1999), Steurer, Smith, and Tracy (2001), and Finn (1998).

REFERENCES

Pastore, Ann L. and Kathleen Maguire, eds. 2007. Sourcebook of Criminal Justice Statistics [Online]. Table 6.28.2005. Available: http://www.albany.edu/sourcebook/. Accessed September 30, 2007.

Finn, Peter. 1998. Texas's Project RIO (Re-Integration of Offenders). Washington DC: National Institute of Justice. NCJ 168637.

Freeman, Richard B. 1992. "Crime and the Employment of Disadvantaged Youth."Pp. 20 1–37 in Urban Labor Markets and Job Opportunity, edited by George Peterson and Wayne Vroman. Washington, DC: Urban Institute Press.

Grogger, Jeffrey. 1995. "The Effect of Arrests on the Employment and Earnings of Young Men." Quarterly Journal of Economics 110:51–71.

Lott, John R. 1990. "The Effect of Conviction on the Legitimate Income of Criminals." Economics Letters 34:381–385.

Saylor, William G. and Gaes, Gerald G. 1997. ''Training Inmates Through Industrial Work Participation and Vocational and Apprenticeship Instruction." Corrections Management Quarterly 1:32–43.

Saylor, William G. and Gaes, Gerald G. 1999. ''The Differential Effect of Industries and Vocational Training on Post Release Outcome for Ethnic and Racial Groups."Office of Research and Evaluation. Washington DC: Federal Bureau of Prisons.

Steurer, Stephen J., Linda Smith and Alice Tracy. 2001. ''Three State Recidivism Study." Report submitted to the Office of Correctional Education, U.S. Department of Education. Lanham, MD: Correctional Education Association.

Waldfogel, Joel. 1994. ''The Effect of Criminal Conviction on Income and the Trust 'Reposed in the Workmen.''' *Journal of Human Resources* 29:62–81.

Western, Bruce. 2002. ‘‘The Impact of Incarceration on Wage Mobility and Inequality.’’ *American Sociological Review* 67:477–98.

Western, Bruce. 2006. Punishment and Inequality in America. New York: Russell Sage Foundation.

Western, Bruce and Katherine Beckett. 1999. ‘‘How Unregulated is the U.S. Labor Market: The Penal System as a Labor Market Institution.’’ *American Journal of Sociology*, 104:1030–60.

INDEX

A

academic, 43, 58, 79, 88, 135, 138
academics, 21
access, 4, 57, 59, 98, 105, 168, 179, 193
accessibility, 193
accountability, 53, 188, 192
achievement, 24, 153
achievement scores, 24
actuarial, 83
acute, 174
adaptation, 12
addiction, 34, 55, 61, 130, 175
adjudications, 49
adjustment, 4, 10
administration, 40
administrative, 8, 57, 70
adolescents, 154
adult, 25, 29, 34, 47, 51, 56, 99, 108, 168, 175, 183
adult convictions, 57
adults, 25, 32, 39, 82, 87, 116, 117, 139, 142, 154, 158, 188, 192
Africa, 96, 163, 196
African American, 75, 76, 78, 93, 96, 97, 116, 134, 137, 154, 163, 164, 166, 195, 196
African Americans, 75, 76, 134
African-American, 134, 198
after-school, 85
age, 33, 77, 92, 96, 98, 129, 135, 150, 152, 154, 163, 165, 168, 169, 197
aid, 103, 130, 171
air, 93
Alabama, 110
Alaska, 198
alcohol, 55, 171
alternative, 24, 46, 93, 100, 123, 124, 131
alternatives, 52, 53, 77, 79, 105, 124, 137, 138, 179, 182
American Society of Criminology, 70
amphetamine, 155
anger, 108, 120, 184
apartheid, 196
application, 35, 48, 52
appropriations, 27, 36, 38, 40, 44, 45, 51, 54, 55, 57
appropriations bills, 45
arithmetic, 84
Arizona, 65
arrest, 12, 42, 93, 94, 111, 113, 117, 122, 123, 125, 140, 154, 155, 158, 161, 162, 169, 187
assessment, 25, 49, 52, 58, 177
assessment tools, 49
atmosphere, 111
attachment, 19, 42, 153
Attorney General, 25, 38, 48, 149
authority, 7, 28, 62, 70, 101
availability, 20, 36, 51, 54, 171, 190
averaging, 13

B

backpack, 80
bail, 16, 122, 123
barriers, 76, 79, 105, 134, 138, 180, 185
base rate, 22
behavior, 77, 94, 117, 118, 124, 135, 149, 158, 177, 191
benefits, 38, 59, 76, 77, 79, 98, 99, 100, 128, 134, 136, 138, 168, 170, 172, 174, 175
bipartisan, 81, 86, 147
birth, 83, 143, 151, 164, 176, 177
Blacks, 93, 94, 96, 97, 150, 154, 158, 162, 163, 195
blame, 90, 117, 148
bleeding, 108, 184
block grants, 29, 32
bodily injury, 70
bonding, 33, 98
bonds, 79, 120, 138
BOP, 35, 36, 57, 58, 59, 62, 192
Boston, 88, 135
breakdown, 94
breeding, 192
Bronx, 114
Brooklyn, 79, 114, 138
buildings, 125
Bureau of the Census, 56

C

candidates, 177
capacity, 106, 180, 181
Capacity, 68
capacity building, 106, 180, 181
capitalism, 88
category a, 22
Catholic, 79, 138
causation, 116
cell, 160
Census, 56, 64, 165
Census Bureau, 165
certificate, 127
certifications, 39
Chad, 70
channels, 167
child bearing, 149
child welfare, 48, 61
childbearing, 164
children, 19, 43, 60, 61, 79, 83, 87, 92, 100, 101, 116, 119, 120, 138, 141, 143, 153, 171, 175, 190
China, 82, 90, 142, 147
citizens, x, 1, 3, 5, 21, 74, 77, 90, 91, 108, 132, 135, 142, 147, 148, 174, 175, 184, 186, 196
classes, 4, 26, 127
clients, 71
clusters, 56
Co, 120, 194
cocaine, 95, 126, 154
codes, 131
cognitive, 25, 58, 153
cohort, 151
collaboration, 48, 55
collateral, 98, 100, 168, 170, 175
Colorado, 65
Columbia, 114, 130, 157
Columbia University, 114, 130, 157
combined effect, 97, 167
Committee on the Judiciary, 34, 69
communication, 61
communities, ix, x, 2, 3, 6, 7, 13, 20, 24, 27, 29, 31, 32, 33, 46, 48, 49, 74, 78, 82, 83, 85, 92, 98, 99, 105, 106, 108, 109, 111, 117, 118, 119, 124, 133, 137, 142, 143, 144, 151, 159, 160, 167, 169, 176, 180, 181, 182, 183, 184, 185, 187, 190, 191, 194, 198
community, ix, 1, 3, 4, 5, 6, 7, 8, 9, 10, 12, 13, 19, 20, 21, 22, 23, 25, 26, 27, 29, 30, 33, 34, 37, 38, 39, 41, 42, 45, 46, 47, 48, 51, 55, 56, 58, 59, 60, 62, 63, 83, 89, 93, 98, 99, 101, 104, 106, 108, 109, 110, 111, 113, 116, 123, 124, 130, 132, 140, 154, 168, 174, 175, 179, 180, 182, 184, 185, 187, 188, 189, 190, 191, 192, 194, 197
Community Development Block Grant, 33

Community Oriented Policing Services, (COPS), 30, 67
community service, 37, 197
community support, 20
community-based services, 26
components, 35
composition, 75, 133, 134, 169
compounds, 172
concentration, 96, 114, 157, 163
concrete, 94, 95, 189
confidence, 66
confinement, 58, 59, 62
confusion, 44
Congress, v, xi, 2, 22, 34, 35, 37, 40, 41, 42, 43, 44, 45, 46, 55, 57, 64, 66, 67, 73, 81, 85, 86, 87, 89, 98, 99, 111, 136, 145, 168, 171, 172, 174, 196
consensus, 42, 104, 179, 192
consent, 35, 52
constraints, 42
construction, ix, 76, 84, 134, 140, 144
consulting, 14
consumption, 93
continuity, 53
contracts, 62
control, 24, 35, 44, 56, 61, 67, 90, 109, 110, 112, 146, 159, 185, 186
controlled substance, 122
conviction, 17, 18, 42, 96, 130, 166, 172
COPS, 30, 67
correlation, ix, 74, 133
corrosive, 117
costs, ix, 3, 18, 19, 26, 57, 75, 77, 79, 82, 83, 84, 86, 102, 105, 107, 119, 123, 129, 130, 133, 136, 138, 140, 142, 143, 144, 179, 196
counsel, 112
counseling, 3, 38, 39, 48, 79, 138
counterfeiting, 120
courts, 18, 19, 36, 51
crack, 126
crime, ix, 5, 7, 14, 15, 16, 22, 23, 35, 37, 53, 59, 70, 74, 75, 76, 77, 78, 81, 82, 83, 84, 85, 86, 90, 104, 105, 106, 107, 112, 115, 117, 120, 124, 126, 127, 128, 129, 131, 132, 133, 134, 137, 140, 142, 143, 144, 145, 146, 148, 157, 158, 159, 160, 170, 172, 174, 179, 180, 181, 182, 183, 190, 191, 192
crimes, 10, 17, 18, 37, 45, 66, 75, 81, 83, 84, 86, 98, 109, 118, 120, 124, 128, 129, 134, 142, 143, 145, 147, 168, 185, 198
criminal activity, 60
criminal behavior, 111, 193
criminal justice, ix, x, 2, 14, 16, 17, 18, 19, 21, 32, 42, 46, 49, 56, 58, 75, 76, 78, 83, 99, 106, 111, 131, 133, 134, 137, 168, 170, 177, 181, 182, 183, 189, 190
criminal justice system, x, 2, 14, 16, 17, 18, 19, 21, 32, 42, 49, 56, 76, 78, 83, 106, 111, 131, 134, 137, 181, 182, 190
criminality, 116
criminals, 30, 58, 75, 84, 90, 114, 120, 128, 133, 144, 148, 159, 191
CRS, 1, 6, 9, 10, 11, 12, 15, 17, 64, 65, 67, 68, 69
crying, 102
cultural factors, 153
Current Population Survey, 165

D

daily living, 39, 58
danger, 190, 197
data collection, 169
data set, 14
database, 14
dating, 126
death, 70, 110, 196
debt, 76, 103, 135
decision making, 123
decisions, 24, 44, 94, 109, 110, 117, 118, 120, 124, 186, 187, 188
defendants, 169
defense, 130
deficit, 172, 174
definition, 10, 14, 17, 18, 21, 51, 62, 115, 120
degrading, 105, 180
delinquent behavior, 83, 143
delinquents, 31
delivery, 26

demand, 36
democracy, 75, 82, 90, 91, 92, 133, 147, 148, 153
demographics, 198
denial, 171, 172, 174
density, 188, 192
Department of Corrections, 65
Department of Education, 33, 41, 69, 200
Department of Health and Human Services, 34, 69
Department of Housing and Urban Development (HUD), 33
Department of Justice (DOJ),, xi, 2, 3, 25, 27, 28, 51, 63, 64, 65, 67, 145
destruction, 113
detention, 5, 21, 29, 59, 60
deterrence, 118, 128, 129
differentiation, 10
diminishing returns, 83, 142
disability, 145
discipline, 92, 153
discretionary, 7, 13, 29, 31, 45, 158
discriminatory, 101, 158
disseminate, 50
dividends, 77, 137
divorce, 116
driver's license, 185
dropouts, 92, 97, 149, 150, 153, 163, 164
drug abuse, 30, 34, 62, 190
drug addict, 131
drug addiction, 131
drug consumption, 157
drug dealing, 131
drug offense, 75, 76, 93, 95, 118, 121, 128, 133, 134, 154
drug sales, 171
drug treatment, 23, 36, 41, 52, 54, 55, 70, 84, 131, 168, 171
drug use, 19, 75, 95, 105, 117, 134, 154, 155, 180
drug-related, 66, 121, 157, 172
drug-resistant, 149
drugs, 19, 55, 70, 93, 95, 113, 117, 118, 121, 122, 125, 126, 130, 155
duplication, 44
duties, 58

E

earnings, 152, 159, 165
earth, 103, 109, 110, 178, 185
economic development, 106, 181
economic growth, ix, 76, 134, 196
economic policy, 131
economic problem, 131
economic stability, 167
economic status, 97, 167
economically disadvantaged, 116
economics, 88
Education, x, 2, 24, 27, 29, 33, 40, 43, 69, 164, 171, 200
educational programs, 41
educational services, 33
elderly, 59, 197
emotional, 92, 153
employability, 32, 130, 159
employees, 125, 189
employers, 32, 100, 166, 171
employment, ix, 4, 19, 20, 23, 30, 37, 39, 75, 76, 79, 89, 97, 98, 100, 101, 105, 108, 109, 123, 125, 131, 133, 134, 135, 138, 145, 152, 165, 166, 167, 168, 171, 175, 179, 182, 184, 186, 189, 199
energy, 77, 135
engines, 106, 181
enterprise, 89
environmental protection, 103, 178
epidemic, 157
epidemiology, 114
ER, 122
ethnicity, 169
Europe, 90, 147
European Union, 198
evacuation, 80
evidence-based program, 83
evil, 120
exaggeration, 92, 153
excuse, 115
expansions, 98, 168
expenditures, ix, 76, 134, 140, 196

expert, v
expertise, 169
eyes, 110, 166, 186

F

failure, 7, 87, 140
fairness, 95
faith, 28, 30, 58, 110, 186, 187, 189, 191, 194
family, 20, 32, 43, 47, 53, 58, 60, 79, 80, 85, 92, 98, 101, 108, 110, 113, 116, 117, 119, 120, 123, 126, 129, 138, 141, 144, 153, 168, 175, 184, 186, 190, 193
family environment, 141
family members, 79, 80, 98, 101, 138, 168, 190
family relationships, 58, 193
family structure, 117
family support, 32
faults, 93
FBI, 17, 170, 183
fear, 111
fears, 91, 148
Federal Bureau of Investigation, 17
federal funds, 35
federal government, x, xi, 2, 20, 25, 26, 40, 41, 44, 46, 134, 140, 196
Federal Prison Industries, 85, 145
feedback, 158
feelings, 186
fees, 190
felony, 52, 70, 85, 92, 96, 145, 151, 157, 171
females, 195
financial institution, 182
financial institutions, 182
fines, 102, 176, 177
firearm, 52, 70
first-time, 123, 198
flight, 126
flow, 126
fluid, 5, 16
focusing, x, 2, 24, 46, 62, 126, 176, 190
food, 170, 172
food stamp, 170, 172
food stamps, 170, 172
FPI, 145
fraud, 130
freedom, 89, 136, 187
frustration, 120
funding, x, xi, 2, 3, 20, 23, 26, 27, 28, 29, 30, 31, 32, 33, 34, 35, 36, 38, 39, 40, 41, 42, 43, 44, 45, 46, 47, 48, 49, 50, 52, 56, 60, 61, 101, 102, 124, 171, 176, 177, 182
funds, 32, 33, 34, 39, 50, 52, 53, 106, 171, 181

G

games, 104, 178
gangs, 76, 132, 135
generation, 92, 153
geriatric, 129
gift, 120
goals, 39, 59
God, 107, 111, 183
government, x, xi, 2, 20, 21, 26, 29, 31, 33, 34, 37, 40, 41, 43, 44, 46, 48, 50, 52, 54, 55, 67, 76, 92, 103, 104, 107, 110, 112, 125, 127, 134, 139, 140, 147, 149, 150, 178, 183, 187, 194, 196, 197, 198, 199
Government Accountability Office (GAO), 4, 63
government expenditure, 197, 198, 199
grants, 25, 26, 29, 31, 32, 35, 36, 37, 48, 49, 50, 51, 52, 53, 54, 55, 56, 61, 79, 81, 138, 171, 187
group activities, 62
groups, 19, 43, 110, 154, 170, 189, 191
growth, ix, 5, 8, 9, 11, 13, 75, 76, 96, 103, 133, 134, 135, 139, 140, 158, 159, 163, 167, 178, 194, 196
growth rate, 8, 9, 13
guidelines, 16, 64, 65
guilty, 7, 123, 183
guns, 125

H

hands, 99

hardships, 141
harm, 70, 118, 130, 183, 191
Harvard, 78, 88, 96, 135, 137, 150, 152, 162
healing, 120
health, 30, 38, 39, 48, 52, 58, 59, 103, 168, 178, 182, 187, 196
Health and Human Services, x, 2, 34, 40, 43, 69
health care, 32, 38, 59, 103, 168, 178, 187, 196
health services, 24, 30, 34, 46, 47, 52
hearing, 74, 77, 79, 80, 81, 86, 87, 88, 99, 111, 112, 120, 121, 122, 130, 132, 136, 138, 139, 141, 146, 183, 194, 196, 199
heart, 191
height, 78, 137, 151
hepatitis, 149
heroin, 61, 95, 154
Heroin, 61
HHS, 34
high risk, 49
high school, 4, 76, 78, 92, 93, 97, 105, 134, 137, 141, 149, 150, 153, 155, 163, 179, 182
higher education, 61, 172
Higher Education Act, 171
high-risk, 25, 32, 46, 58, 59
high-risk populations, 58
hiring, 171
Hispanic, 83, 143, 152, 195
Hispanics, 91, 149, 150, 158, 162
holistic, 193
Holland, 157
Homeland Security, 141
homeless, 100, 175
hospital, 53, 109, 185
hospitals, 108, 184
host, 85, 106, 145, 181
House, 23, 28, 34, 47, 59, 74, 87, 113, 115
House Appropriations Committee, 28
household, 165, 175
housing, x, 2, 3, 23, 25, 30, 31, 32, 33, 38, 39, 41, 46, 47, 48, 51, 56, 76, 98, 100, 101, 105, 111, 134, 168, 171, 172, 174, 175, 176, 177, 179, 185, 191
Housing and Urban Development, 27, 29, 40
housing benefit, 98, 168, 172
HUD, 33
human, 86, 90, 91, 147, 148, 153, 176, 183, 187
human development, 153
humanitarian, 81
humanity, 91, 149
humiliation, 110
hygiene, 40

I

id, 177
Idaho, 126
identification, 58, 176, 186
identity, 18, 75, 133
Illinois, 65
implementation, 35, 38, 48, 52, 53, 57
imprisonment, ix, 7, 52, 58, 74, 77, 79, 83, 90, 91, 96, 97, 121, 133, 136, 138, 142, 148, 149, 151, 152, 158, 159, 160, 163, 164, 165, 167, 183, 196
incarceration, ix, x, 2, 3, 7, 10, 20, 41, 53, 60, 61, 74, 75, 77, 78, 82, 83, 86, 87, 88, 90, 91, 92, 96, 97, 98, 99, 100, 101, 104, 105, 107, 108, 112, 113, 114, 115, 116, 118, 121, 123, 124, 128, 130, 133, 135, 136, 137, 140, 142, 143, 145, 146, 148, 149, 151, 152, 153, 155, 157, 158, 159, 160, 163, 164, 165, 167, 168, 169, 170, 172, 175, 177, 179, 182, 183, 184, 187, 190, 194, 195, 197, 198
incentive, 84, 88, 144, 145, 177
incentives, 26, 32, 58, 98, 107, 145, 168, 181
incidence, 91, 149
income, 130, 172
incomes, 97, 167
India, 82, 142
Indian, 25, 53, 54, 55
Indiana, 70
indicators, 42
industrial, 90, 147, 196
industry, 107, 181
inequality, 88, 94, 135
infant mortality, 97, 149, 164

infant mortality rate, 149
infants, 19
infections, 149
infectious, 149
infectious disease, 149
information sharing, 43
infrastructure, 176, 182, 196
inheritance, 90, 148
injury, v
inmates, 5, 8, 16, 33, 40, 59, 79, 85, 92, 95, 108, 109, 110, 111, 138, 139, 140, 141, 145, 149, 152, 157, 160, 165, 177, 184, 185, 186, 187, 188, 189, 190, 191, 192, 193, 194, 197
innovation, 140, 141
insight, 87, 167
institutions, 33, 43, 46, 149, 193, 194
instruction, 33
instruments, 131
insurance, 33
integration, 47, 167
intensity, 20, 94, 95, 122, 160
Internet, 54
intervention, 30, 31, 83, 143
interview, 22, 64, 109, 186
interviews, 188
investment, 38, 108, 184
isolation, 108, 149, 184
Israel, xi, 73

J

jails, 5, 15, 16, 41, 64, 74, 77, 85, 87, 124, 132, 136, 139, 145, 147, 149, 196, 198
January, 64, 70, 182
Japan, 112, 127
Japanese, 112, 127
job skills, 171
job training, 38, 41, 51, 56, 78, 84, 137, 144, 176, 177
jobless, 165
jobs, 46, 85, 100, 102, 128, 144, 167, 175, 177, 191
judge, 123, 191
judges, 20
Judiciary, 35, 59, 81, 139
Judiciary Committee, 81
jurisdiction, 26
jurisdictions, 64, 99, 168
justice, ix, 18, 31, 46, 58, 68, 89, 99, 102, 124, 130, 133, 136, 163, 170, 177, 182, 183, 189
Justice Assistance Grant, 29, 67
Justice Department, 198
juvenile delinquents, 31
juvenile justice, 31, 68, 89, 136
juveniles, 31, 82, 85, 117, 142, 144

K

kindergarten, 87
King, 110, 188

L

labor, 150, 152, 165, 166, 167
labor force, 165
landscapes, 147
language, 8, 35, 36, 37, 38, 62, 92, 197
Latino, 94, 195
Latinos, 195, 198
law, ix, x, 1, 3, 21, 30, 35, 47, 48, 57, 58, 76, 77, 86, 89, 90, 105, 108, 112, 122, 125, 129, 130, 134, 135, 136, 143, 145, 147, 148, 153, 158, 160, 172, 179, 184, 186, 191, 196
law enforcement, ix, 30, 48, 76, 86, 105, 122, 125, 134, 143, 145, 147, 158, 160, 179, 196
laws, 11, 91, 101, 109, 120, 123, 128, 131, 148, 153, 157, 158, 185
lead, 7, 89, 135, 140, 159, 172, 176, 183
learning, 25
legislation, 87, 139, 140, 196, 197, 198
legislative, 102, 140, 194
liberty, 90, 91, 147, 148
licenses, 185
life course, 92, 152
life cycle, 128
lifecycle, 159
life-threatening, 149

lifetime, 96, 163, 164
likelihood, 17, 60, 123, 187
limitations, 16, 24, 98, 168
links, 92, 153
listening, 100, 112, 122
literacy, 47
loans, 76, 135, 171, 185
local community, 174
local government, 31, 33, 34, 43, 48, 54, 55, 139, 196, 197, 199
location, 22
lockups, 5
logistics, 110, 186
long period, 128
long-term, x, 2, 3, 26, 29, 35, 48, 52, 53, 55
losses, 167
Louisiana, 80
love, 110, 188
low risk, 185
low-income, 172
low-level, 75, 118, 122, 128, 133

M

magnetic, v
Maine, 14
mainstream, 155
maintenance, 91, 100, 148
males, 78, 137, 195, 196
management, 39, 49, 102, 176
Manhattan, 114
marijuana, 94, 122, 126, 154, 158
marital conflict, 190
market, 74, 86, 93, 121, 132, 152, 166, 167
market economy, 74, 132
markets, 126
Maryland, 22, 65
Massachusetts, 30
matching funds, 50, 52, 53
measurement, 22
measures, xi, 3, 16, 18, 19, 22, 23, 24, 26, 39, 42, 46, 48, 50, 52, 56, 84, 95, 131, 143, 165, 168
Medicaid, 103, 178
medications, 70
men, 76, 79, 92, 96, 97, 111, 116, 130, 134, 150, 151, 152, 163, 164, 165, 166, 167, 185, 188, 193, 195
mental health, x, 2, 21, 24, 25, 32, 34, 39, 46, 56, 58, 59, 78, 137, 149
mental illness, x, 2, 105, 180
mentor, 188, 189
mentoring, 36, 37, 47, 54, 55, 56, 79, 110, 138, 188, 192
mentoring program, 36, 47, 54, 55, 110
methamphetamine, 95
metric, 19
Mexico, 74, 125, 132
microeconomic theory, 88, 135
middle class, 157
middle-aged, 197
military, 97, 130, 164
minimum wage, 100
Minnesota, 65
minorities, 83, 118, 143
minority, ix, 74, 83, 98, 99, 133, 143, 160, 167, 169, 198
mirror, 153
Missouri, 30
mobility, 167
models, 177
money, ix, 76, 79, 84, 93, 102, 103, 104, 105, 106, 109, 118, 119, 125, 134, 143, 144, 159, 178, 180, 186, 187
Montana, 126
mood, 75, 133
moral identity, 75, 133
moral standards, 191
morality, 191
morning, 81, 103, 136, 178
mortality, 97, 149, 164
mothers, 79, 138
motion, 34
motives, 125
movement, 121
multidisciplinary, 88
mutual respect, 193

N

nation, 5, 103, 138, 178, 180, 196, 198
national, x, xi, 1, 3, 5, 14, 15, 39, 41, 45, 46, 60, 77, 90, 91, 94, 99, 104, 130, 135, 147, 148, 149, 155, 158, 179
National Academy of Sciences, 16
National Crime Victimization Survey, 170
National Incident-Based Reporting System, 170
natural, 20
negative consequences, 170
network, 189
New Jersey, 65
New Mexico, 74, 132
New York, iii, vi, 65, 77, 78, 89, 94, 105, 106, 114, 119, 120, 136, 137, 157, 158, 160, 161, 162, 180, 182, 187, 190, 200
New York Times, 78, 137
NIC, 31
non-profit, 20, 34, 38, 39, 43, 49, 56, 141, 187
non-violent, 37, 53, 59, 128, 147, 160, 174, 185, 197, 198
Norfolk, 88, 89, 100, 101, 124, 135, 174, 175
normal, 97, 120, 164
norms, 160
North Carolina, 65
nursing, 102

O

obligations, 176, 177
observations, 93, 127, 154, 183
occupational, 128
offenders, ix, x, 1, 2, 3, 4, 5, 6, 7, 8, 9, 10, 12, 13, 14, 16, 17, 18, 19, 21, 23, 24, 25, 27, 29, 30, 31, 32, 33, 34, 35, 36, 37, 38, 39, 40, 41, 42, 45, 46, 47, 48, 49, 51, 52, 53, 54, 55, 56, 57, 58, 59, 60, 61, 62, 63, 64, 66, 75, 76, 78, 79, 84, 86, 89, 90, 91, 95, 100, 101, 102, 103, 109, 128, 133, 134, 136, 137, 138, 141, 143, 145, 148, 149, 159, 160, 166, 175, 176, 177, 183, 184, 185, 186, 187, 188, 189, 190, 192, 196, 197, 198
Office of Justice Programs (OJP), 27, 28, 29, 38, 63, 67, 68
Office of Juvenile Justice and Delinquency Prevention (OJJDP), 31
Office of Vocational and Adult Education, 33
Ohio, 15, 63, 65, 170
OJP, 29, 30
opportunity costs, 84
oral, 40
oral hygiene, 40
Oregon, 65
organization, 50
organizations, 20, 30, 34, 37, 38, 39, 43, 49, 56, 58, 141, 192
organized crime, 128
orientation, 177
outpatient, 53
oversight, 25, 40, 44

P

pandemic, 128
paper, 128
Paper, 63, 70
pardons, 12
parent-child, 61
parenting, 39, 175, 193
parents, 53, 60, 61, 100, 175
parole, 6, 7, 8, 9, 10, 11, 12, 13, 14, 16, 19, 20, 34, 37, 49, 60, 61, 64, 74, 75, 82, 83, 84, 85, 101, 133, 139, 142, 143, 145, 177, 194
parole board, 7, 13, 177
partnership, 27, 187
partnerships, 56
paternal, 115
patients, 109, 185
pay off, 102
peer, 102
peer support, 102
Pell Grants, 171
penalties, 98, 167
per capita, 158

perception, 118
performance, 49, 50, 56, 141
personal, 110, 111, 123, 186, 189, 193
personal problems, 189
petitioners, 37
pharmacological, 36, 55
pharmacotherapies, 62
phone, 119, 193
physical abuse, 190
physical health, 47, 159
pilot programs, xi, 2, 36, 45, 101, 176
pilots, 177
piracy, 120
planning, 4, 26, 35, 36, 39, 58, 61, 71, 101, 102, 175, 176, 177, 190
play, 18, 82, 122, 142
police, 18, 92, 94, 114, 122, 123, 124, 125, 126, 131, 150, 157, 158, 169, 170, 182, 191
policy initiative, 90, 148
policy makers, 19, 21, 23, 24, 42, 44, 45
policymakers, 107, 140, 170, 181
politeness, 189
politics, 82, 83, 107, 142, 143, 181, 182
poor, 39, 97, 98, 99, 116, 117, 119, 131, 166, 167, 168, 171, 174, 175
population, ix, 1, 3, 4, 5, 8, 9, 10, 11, 12, 13, 16, 22, 42, 45, 49, 50, 53, 60, 62, 75, 76, 78, 82, 91, 94, 96, 97, 103, 105, 106, 112, 113, 116, 117, 119, 133, 134, 137, 139, 140, 142, 149, 157, 163, 165, 166, 171, 178, 179, 180, 194, 196, 197, 198
population growth, 5
positive feedback, 158
postsecondary education, 33
powder, 126
power, 22, 90, 146
predators, 193
prediction, 16
predictors, 190
president, 89, 107
President Bush, 81, 113, 196
pressure, 45, 160
pretrial, 169
prevention, 24, 30, 39, 46, 84, 106, 143, 144, 180
preventive, 39
PRI, 27, 28, 29, 30
prices, 121, 155, 157
prisoners, ix, 3, 5, 6, 11, 12, 13, 15, 19, 20, 36, 41, 54, 55, 56, 58, 62, 76, 84, 96, 98, 108, 111, 119, 129, 134, 144, 149, 159, 163, 165, 167, 168, 182, 184, 187, 188, 190, 192, 193, 194, 197, 198, 199
prisons, 5, 12, 15, 20, 55, 64, 74, 75, 76, 77, 80, 84, 85, 87, 103, 106, 108, 109, 118, 119, 124, 125, 127, 128, 129, 132, 133, 134, 136, 139, 143, 144, 145, 147, 149, 159, 178, 181, 182, 184, 185, 190, 192, 194, 196, 198
private, 20, 39, 61, 63, 107, 117, 125, 181
probability, 66
probation, 6, 7, 8, 10, 12, 13, 14, 16, 34, 61, 74, 89, 101, 133, 139, 191, 194
probation officers, 7, 61
productivity, ix, 76, 134
profit, 20, 34, 38, 39, 43, 49, 56, 141
profits, 187
program, x, xi, 2, 18, 19, 21, 22, 24, 25, 26, 27, 28, 29, 30, 31, 32, 34, 35, 36, 37, 38, 39, 42, 43, 45, 48, 49, 50, 51, 52, 53, 54, 55, 56, 57, 58, 59, 60, 62, 67, 69, 70, 78, 79, 85, 88, 98, 100, 102, 110, 120, 124, 135, 137, 138, 140, 145, 150, 174, 175, 188, 191
programming, x, 1, 3, 21, 182, 192
promote, 26, 47, 63, 99, 176
property, v, 147
property crimes, 147
prosecutor, 52, 126
protection, 103, 178
public, ix, 39, 45, 54, 61, 62, 74, 75, 76, 77, 78, 79, 86, 90, 92, 94, 98, 99, 102, 104, 105, 106, 107, 111, 112, 114, 117, 118, 128, 129, 130, 132, 133, 134, 135, 136, 137, 138, 140, 141, 145, 148, 150, 159, 168, 170, 171, 172, 174, 178, 179, 180, 181, 185, 190, 193, 196
public housing, 105, 172, 174, 179, 185
public investment, 196
public policy, 45, 74, 132

public safety, ix, 54, 76, 77, 79, 98, 99, 104, 106, 118, 128, 129, 134, 136, 138, 140, 141, 159, 168, 171, 172, 174, 178, 179, 180, 181, 193, 196
public sector, 92, 150
punishment, 91, 95, 99, 102, 103, 107, 124, 129, 148, 149, 181, 195
punitive, 78, 124, 131, 137

R

race, 91, 93, 94, 151, 154, 169, 195
racketeering, 183
random, 16, 24, 49, 66
random assignment, 24, 49
range, x, 2, 3, 20, 23, 39, 41, 64, 66, 165, 166, 170
rape, 108, 184
reading, 93, 119, 131
reality, 83, 92, 125, 143, 153
rearrest, 14, 15, 17, 185, 187
recidivate, 3, 17, 42, 60
recidivism, x, xi, 1, 3, 14, 15, 16, 17, 18, 19, 23, 24, 27, 33, 38, 40, 41, 42, 45, 46, 49, 56, 59, 60, 63, 64, 65, 75, 80, 81, 85, 86, 98, 100, 109, 133, 140, 141, 145, 168, 172, 176, 193
recidivism rate, 3, 14, 16, 56, 59, 60, 75, 80, 81, 85, 100, 133, 141, 145
reconcile, 120
reconviction, 14, 15, 17
recovery, 55
reduction, 84, 131, 143, 167, 182, 197
reforms, 13, 169, 170
regular, 7, 75, 134
regulation, 117
regulations, 51, 120, 197
rehabilitate, 159
rehabilitation, 23, 84, 98, 143, 144, 167, 171
rehabilitation program, 84, 143, 144
relapse, 23, 176
relationship, 10, 12, 16, 103, 175, 178
relationships, 58, 188, 190, 192, 193
relatives, 93
repair, 127, 183
Republican, 89, 107, 136, 139, 183
Republicans, 139
rescission, 28
research, x, 2, 4, 46, 60, 61, 62, 64, 83, 84, 97, 99, 105, 106, 113, 121, 131, 143, 169, 179, 181, 182
researchers, 14, 22, 66
residential, 31, 50, 53, 62, 157, 169, 170, 171
resolution, 112, 127
resources, 4, 23, 27, 29, 30, 43, 44, 49, 77, 101, 105, 106, 118, 128, 130, 137, 169, 170, 180, 182
responsibilities, 58, 79, 138
restitution, 48, 176
Restorative Justice, 63
retail, 155, 157
retention, 100, 175
retribution, 129
returns, 142
revenue, 197
risk, x, 2, 25, 32, 42, 46, 48, 49, 59, 60, 83, 109, 110, 116, 122, 125, 142, 143, 151, 177, 185, 193
risk assessment, 48
risk factors, x, 2, 177
risks, 123, 164
rolling, 123
RTI, 67
RTI International, 67
rural, ix, 76, 106, 134, 147, 181
rural communities, ix, 76, 106, 134, 181
Russia, 82, 90, 96, 142, 147, 163

S

safeguard, 61
safety, 61, 106, 125, 129, 171, 179, 180, 190
sales, 75, 128, 133, 171
sample, 16, 22
sanctions, 7, 26, 53, 60, 194
satellite, 59
scandalous, 91, 150
scarce resources, 105, 130, 180
scholarships, 85, 144

school, 4, 21, 76, 78, 85, 92, 93, 97, 102, 105, 108, 119, 134, 137, 141, 144, 149, 150, 153, 155, 163, 179, 182, 184, 187
schooling, 96, 163, 166, 169
scientists, 104, 179
scores, 24
secondary education, 39, 104, 172, 178
security, 48
seed, 30
selecting, 177
Senate, xi, 35, 38, 47, 59, 73, 85, 139, 145, 185
sentences, 4, 5, 6, 7, 8, 10, 11, 12, 13, 15, 16, 18, 20, 59, 78, 79, 82, 85, 108, 109, 129, 131, 137, 138, 142, 145, 184, 185, 197
sentencing, 4, 8, 11, 13, 16, 64, 65, 75, 109, 124, 127, 133, 158, 169, 170, 185
Sentencing Guidelines, 64, 65
separation, 116
series, 39, 54, 81, 113, 115
services, v, x, 2, 3, 13, 20, 24, 25, 26, 29, 30, 31, 32, 33, 34, 36, 37, 38, 39, 41, 44, 45, 46, 47, 49, 50, 51, 53, 55, 56, 57, 60, 63, 71, 85, 89, 98, 100, 101, 102, 103, 135, 140, 161, 162, 168, 171, 175, 176, 177, 178, 182
severity, 127, 131
sex, 24, 57, 58, 59, 169
sex offenders, 24
sexual abuse, 78, 137
shadow economy, 131
sharing, 43
short period, 125
sites, 176
skills, 4, 21, 32, 33, 39, 58, 102, 108, 111, 127, 145, 153, 166, 171, 177, 184, 186, 189, 193
skills training, 102, 193
smoking, 94
sobriety, 43, 125
social class, 151
social costs, 77, 136
social group, 169
social indicator, 97, 164
social institutions, 19
social life, 149
social network, 42
social policy, 88
social problems, 91
Social Security, 197
social services, 20, 103, 178
social status, 116
social welfare, 149
socioeconomic, 99, 168
sociologist, 78, 137, 150, 152, 158
sociologists, 114
solutions, 87, 115
South Africa, 96, 163, 196
spatial, 114, 157
spawning, 192
spills, 192
spiritual, 91, 193
spouse, 120
St. Louis, 22
stability, 89, 113, 135, 153, 167
stages, 39
stakeholders, 43, 170
standards, 141, 191
statistics, xi, 3, 6, 14, 17, 18, 40, 41, 59, 94, 113, 117, 158, 165, 167
statutes, 109, 158
statutory, 7, 8, 48, 120
stigma, 83, 89, 116, 135, 142, 160, 166
strain, 103, 178, 187, 197, 199
strategic, 35, 48, 49
strategies, 38, 55, 140, 182
strength, 116
stress, 106, 110, 116, 180, 186, 190
strikes, 159
structural changes, 13
students, 172
substance abuse, x, 2, 21, 23, 24, 25, 34, 37, 39, 41, 46, 47, 48, 50, 52, 53, 55, 56, 70, 71, 79, 108, 111, 138, 175, 184, 193
substances, 93, 95
suburban, 117
summaries, 74
summer, 79, 85, 138, 144
supervised release, 108, 183

supervision, x, 1, 2, 3, 6, 7, 8, 9, 12, 13, 16, 20, 30, 31, 34, 44, 47, 55, 59, 60, 61, 74, 78, 109, 133, 137, 139, 140, 185, 194
supervisor, 189
suppliers, 94
supply, 18
support services, 30, 50, 55, 56, 88, 135
support staff, 176
surprise, 93, 187
surveillance, 193
survival, 171
systems, 3, 13, 20, 21, 41, 51, 102, 104, 105, 139, 160, 179, 180, 191

T

tactics, 124
TANF, 170, 172
targets, 34
tax credit, 33
tax credits, 33
taxpayers, 140, 187
technical assistance, 31, 50, 57
technology, 54, 193
teenagers, 158
telephone, 70, 190
tenure, 167
testimony, 86, 88, 90, 95, 112, 113, 114, 115, 121, 122, 132, 136, 146, 148, 159, 169, 170, 176, 177, 181
Texas, 65, 188, 194, 196, 198
therapists, 25
thinking, 111, 125, 194
threat, 104, 106, 124, 157, 160, 179, 181
threats, 104, 179
time, 4, 5, 9, 10, 11, 14, 16, 21, 22, 40, 58, 76, 79, 80, 86, 88, 89, 93, 96, 97, 98, 102, 106, 110, 112, 114, 118, 121, 123, 125, 126, 127, 128, 129, 130, 131, 132, 134, 135, 138, 139, 140, 143, 153, 154, 157, 158, 163, 164, 166, 168, 176, 180, 186, 187, 188, 189, 191, 197, 198
time commitment, 188
time frame, 14
title, 128
tracking, 59
trade, 117
training, x, 2, 3, 4, 24, 25, 31, 32, 33, 36, 38, 39, 41, 46, 50, 52, 54, 56, 78, 79, 84, 102, 108, 111, 137, 138, 144, 175, 176, 177, 184, 191, 193
training programs, 36, 54
transfer, 62, 106, 180
transformation, 95, 111, 193
transition, 19, 21, 23, 29, 39, 41, 56, 79, 102, 109, 138, 175, 185, 186, 188, 192
transparency, 193
transportation, 103, 177, 178
treason, 120
treatment programs, 25, 40, 50, 52, 53, 54, 55, 171
trend, 13, 106, 121, 146, 154, 181
tribal, 34
tribes, 25
tuberculosis, 149
tuition, 78, 137
tutoring, 100

U

unemployment, 97, 102, 149, 164, 165
unemployment rate, 149
Uniform Crime Reports, 170
unions, 107, 149, 181
United Kingdom, 5, 54
United States, i, iii, vii, ix, xi, 1, 3, 5, 16, 17, 18, 38, 59, 62, 63, 65, 66, 73, 74, 77, 78, 82, 83, 87, 90, 91, 103, 104, 107, 108, 111, 112, 125, 128, 132, 133, 136, 142, 146, 147, 148, 178, 181, 183, 184, 194, 195, 196, 198
universe, 19, 27
universities, 78, 137
upward mobility, 167
urban areas, 117, 131
urbanized, 56

V

values, 91, 148
variables, 22
variation, 66
vein, 105, 179
veterans, 38
Vice President, 107, 183
victimization, 106, 180
victims, 48, 49, 56, 86, 104, 130, 145, 170, 179, 183, 187, 190, 191
Vietnam, 151
Vietnam War, 151
vineyard, 86
violence, 37, 57, 70, 75, 83, 108, 109, 133, 143, 174, 184, 185, 192
violent, 16, 24, 30, 31, 51, 57, 59, 70, 76, 84, 91, 106, 118, 134, 135, 143, 148, 149, 180, 185, 197, 198
violent behavior, 77, 135
violent crime, 16, 30, 76, 84, 106, 118, 134, 144, 180, 185, 197
violent crimes, 16, 76, 118, 134, 185
violent offenders, 24, 31, 37, 59, 174, 185, 197, 198
vocational, 4, 23, 24, 25, 33, 41, 46, 47, 54, 58, 79, 85, 108, 111, 145, 184, 193
vocational education, 79
vocational training, 4, 24, 25, 33, 41, 46, 111, 193
voluntary unemployment, 102
voting, 92, 153
vouchers, 177

W

wages, 97, 105, 152, 159, 165, 167, 179, 182
Wall Street Journal, 159
war, 147, 155
warehousing, 197, 199
Washington Post, 75, 133
wealth, 97, 164
weapons, 37
web, 63
welfare, 48, 61, 98, 150, 168, 171, 174
welfare reform, 171
well-being, 165
Western Europe, 96, 163
White House, 113
wind, 105, 118, 180
wisdom, 87
witnesses, 74, 77, 86, 89, 132, 135, 136, 141
women, ix, 75, 78, 79, 111, 133, 137, 171, 175, 185, 188, 193
workers, 167
workforce, 32, 38
Workforce Investment Act, 32, 33, 68
workplace, 4, 189
World War, 151
World War I, 151
World War II, 151
worry, 110, 186
Wyoming, 198

Y

young adults, 39, 87, 158
young men, 96, 130, 163, 167

Z

zero sum game, 178